Dat

THE GUILTY AND
THE INNOCENT

In this remarkable book William Bixley,
for fifty years a supervisory official of the
Central Criminal Court, tells the tempestuous
story of the Old Bailey. He describes the
horrifying tortures and punishments of the
Court's early history, recalls outstanding scenes
from the past, and then devotes the main body
of his book to his personal memories of the
most sensational trials of this century. Murderers, gangsters, financial tricksters, arsonists,
spies judged in the secret trials of both World
Wars, sexual sadists—he saw them all in their
struggles for life or death. In taking the
reader behind the scenes, into chambers where
the public is forbidden, and into a proximity
with the greatest advocates of our time which
no ordinary person can ever achieve, the tense
drama of these court room battles is brought
enthrallingly alive. No thrillers of fiction can
match the extraordinary cases that have taken
place inside Old Bailey, and few people have
been in such a privileged position to witness
them as William Bixley.

THE
Guilty
AND THE
Innocent

MY FIFTY YEARS
AT THE OLD BAILEY

By

WILLIAM BIXLEY

PHILOSOPHICAL LIBRARY • NEW YORK

Published, 1957, by Philosophical Library, Inc.,
15 East 40th Street, New York 16, N.Y.

Printed in Great Britain for Philosophical Library
by The Central Press, Aberdeen.

CONTENTS

1. THE OLD BAILEY   9

2. INFAMOUS OLD BAILEY CRIMINALS   25

3. "NOT GUILTY!"   33

4. THE METHODS OF THE POISONER   45

5. THE FATAL GLITTER OF GOLD   58

6. TRIALS FOR ESPIONAGE AND TREACHERY   76

7. WOMEN WHO FACED THE BRAND OF CAIN   95

8. THE MANIA OF MURDER   111

9. PEOPLE WITH GUNS   138

10. SOME STRANGE CASES   154

11. UPHOLDING THE LAW   170

ILLUSTRATIONS

Between pages 48 and 49.

The Central Criminal Court, Old Bailey, 1841†.

The torture of " pressing " for non-pleaders†.

The last dying speech of two unfortunate malefactors†.

A mass execution at the New Gallows in the Old Bailey†.

Between pages 112 and 113.

Frederick Bywaters arriving at Ilford Court, 1922‡.

Crowds outside the Old Bailey await the result of the Thompson-Bywaters trial†.

Mrs. Edith Thompson—murderess*.

Mrs. Elvira Barney—innocent*.

Horatio Bottomley, self-styled Friend of the Poor, is brought to Bow Street, 1921†.

Dr. Crippen†.

John George Haigh*.

Neville George Clevely Heath*.

John Reginald Halliday Christie*.

Christie and the Notting Hill murders: the back garden of No. 10 Rillington Place, where police dug for remains of victims*.

CHAPTER ONE

The Old Bailey

"ALL PERSONS HAVING ANYTHING TO DO before my Lords the Queen's Justices of Oyer and Terminer and general gaol delivery, for the jurisdiction of the Central Criminal Court, held here this day by adjournment, draw near and give your attendance. God save the Queen."

Over and over again during the fifty years that I worked at the Old Bailey I have heard the solemn introduction.

Yet fifty years are a mere episode in the period that a similar announcement has been made that justice is about to be done in this historic site of law and justice. The Central Criminal Court came into being in 1834, but for centuries before that date this western corner of the City of London had been the scene where the law of the land was administered. Very probably rough justice was provided here, and the guilty imprisoned, before the beginning of the Christian era, when London was merely a collection of huts on the north side of the boggy, meandering Thames.

When the Romans came to London they found a gate in the vicinity, and they rebuilt it on two occasions, as was proved during the excavations for the construction of the present building, which began in 1902. There was a strongly fortified Roman gate on the site of the Old Bailey when Ludgate was a mere postern, and although in later centuries its regular reconstruction gave it the name of Newgate it was probably the first of the defended entrances to the City of London.

In early times it was known as Westgate, and when anyone was imprisoned in the strong house built alongside he was said to have "gone west", which may well have been the origin of the universal saying of today.

In the tenth century a group of civic laws, *Judicia Civitatis Lundonie,* gave the authorities of the City of London the right to exercise criminal jurisdiction. This privilege has been jealously guarded ever since. When William the Conqueror became King he agreed, as the price of London's surrender, to permit the continuance of its legal customs. Henry I, about 1132, issued a Charter granting the citizens of London the right to appoint " whom they would of themselves for keeping pleas of the Crown and that none other should be justice over them ".

Even today the Lord Mayor of London is the Chief Magistrate of the City and is the first-named judge in the Act of 1834 which created the Central Criminal Court.

He attends every session of the Court, and his privileges at the Old Bailey mean that he takes precedence even over the Lord Chancellor, thus preserving a memory of the ancient rights of the citizens that none other than the citizens' choice should be in justice over them.

By the thirteenth century Newgate prison, as it was by that time called, was gaining a terrible reputation. It was generally known as a heynhouse (hated house). On various occasions the monarch ordered the City authorities to put repairs in hand and in the will of Dick Whittington, the famous Lord Mayor of London who died in 1421, although there was no specific order that the money should be used to improve the condition of the prisoners, his direction that his considerable fortune should be devoted to good works resulted in the prison being largely rebuilt. At this time also the site ceased to be a City gate.

Up to then the trials of the prisoners were held, either in the open or in any convenient private house or tavern, by the Court of Hustings which every citizen was allowed to attend. The earliest one is believed to have been held on the high ground on which the General Post Office now stands. In 1539 the first Court was erected. At this period, prisoners were brought to trial only once a year and in their resolution the Court of Aldermen stated that they intended to build a house for trying Newgate prisoners.

" This house should be built over and against Flete Lane
in the Olde Bayley with gardens for the health and pleasure
of the Justices."

No earlier reference to the now famous name of the
Central Criminal Court has been discovered. It is quite
obvious from the matter-of-fact way in which the term was
included in this resolution that it was the normal description used by the citizens of London for the narrow lane
which led to Newgate prison.

Its origin probably comes from the Roman word
" ballium ", which signifies a defence wall, or else from
the fact that there had long been an open space nearby
where the bailiffs tried their prisoners.

The first Sessions House was burned down during the
Great Fire of London in 1666. The original Sessions House
was, of course, quite small, and in view of the notoriety of
the adjoining prison, it is the history of that place which
has the most remarkable story to tell.

When the prison was rebuilt after its destruction in the
Fire of London it was designed to hold three hundred male
prisoners, a hundred debtors, and sixty women. It was
nearly always overcrowded, and when a census was taken
in 1809, there were nearly eight hundred there. Eight years
later the gaol's population reached a thousand, including
several hundred children.

The punishments administered to the guilty at this time
were frightful indeed. Up to 1700 treason brought the
penalty of hanging, drawing and quartering, the last being
achieved by harnessing horses to the prisoners' limbs.
Murder by poison was punishable by being boiled to death.
A man named Rouse, who poisoned twenty people when
attempting to murder the Archbishop of Rochester, was
boiled alive in Smithfield in 1561—the scene of the execution fires of religious criminals.

Writers of libellous matter had their hands cut off by a
cleaver driven through the wrists by blows from a mallet.
There is the record of a man who was thus punished during
the reign of Elizabeth I who bravely plucked off his hat

with his uninjured hand, and shouted " God save the Queen ". Seditious writing or speeches were punished by branding the forehead, slitting the nose, and cutting off the ears. It was quite common for some men to be sentenced to be put in the pillory and to have their ears nailed to the woodwork so that they could only get themselves free by tearing the ears away.

A still more ghastly form of punishment was that administered in the Press Yard. Pressing was the sentence pronounced on any one who refused to plead, and there were cases where some unfortunate deaf-and-dumb person had to undergo it. The most famous account of the punishment of a prisoner by pressing concerned Major Strangeways who was sentenced in 1657 by Lord Chief Justice Glynn. He was laid on his back, his body clothed only in a white gown, with his arms and legs stretched outwards by cords. The first day he was given three pieces of dry bread and on the next three sips of water, while iron bars and stones were laid on his body. The intention of this punishment was not to kill the prisoner, but to break down his resistance and make him plead. In the case of Major Strangeways, who had been found guilty of murder, his friends outwitted justice by climbing on to his chest to crush his ribs and cause his death. Pressing was abandoned in 1715 when thumb screws replaced it.

Whipping was a normal punishment for all sorts of minor and major crimes, ranging from begging and wandering without visible means of support to an extra punishment for the most serious misdemeanours. The infamous Titus Oates, who was indicted for perjury and tried at the Old Bailey by the notorious Judge Jeffreys, was lashed two thousand times, for the last few hundred of which he was, fortunately for him, unconscious.

Not all the prisoners suffered these diabolical punishments. Some seem to have merely remained in prison almost forgotten. There is the record of a man towards the end of the seventeenth century, Major Fernardio, who was imprisoned during the reign of William and Mary in Newgate on suspicion of being a traitor. He lived quite happily in the gaol for more than forty years. He got married while he was there and became the father of ten children. He died at the ripe old age of eighty-two—still a prisoner.

In the same year that the gallant Major died, there was the first recorded instance of the execution of a criminal at the Old Bailey. It took place on December 22, 1690, and the victim was a woman, Ann Hereford, charged with robbery and arson. Ann was one of the most infamous criminals of her day, who usually dressed as a man and could fight with her fists or with a sword with such skill and strength that few people accepted the fact that she was indeed a woman. The reason that she was executed at Newgate, instead of at Tyburn or in Smithfield, was that she set fire to the prison while awaiting trial for robbery and she was hanged in the sight of the other prisoners as an example.

Throughout the eighteenth century Newgate was a hell on earth. Some idea of the corruption which prevailed may be gained from the fact that as early as 1696 the Keeper of Newgate paid £3,500 to obtain his post—a sum not far short of £60,000 in modern money.

The racketeering which prevailed varied, of course, as the years went by, but a detailed description of the prison as it was in the early 1700's was fairly typical of the conditions that existed until Queen Victoria came to the throne.

When the prisoner was escorted by bailiffs or the Sheriff's representatives to the gaol entrance, he was first of all taken to a small lodge where he was fettered unless he paid a fee to avoid this. This extortion was called "easement money". Even the corrupt officials of Newgate did not, of course, try to fetter the prisoners who were merely there for debt, but these prisoners were still held to ransom by being taken to a windowless room with rings all around the walls. To avoid being chained to these rings and to get out of the pitch-black room a fee of 2s. 6d. had to be paid.

The better class of debtor could then get into the accommodation on the Master Debtors' side, where there was an enormous room with tiers of wooden benches all around the sides. On these benches, for a fee of 2s. 6d. per week, he could obtain a space and a mattress. Sheets cost 2s. per week extra. The last prisoner to be admitted each day had to clean the whole place or pay 2d. a week to some prisoner from the Felons' side to do it for him. The official ration for debtors was one loaf per person per day with some beef on Sundays, but it was very simple to obtain as much food and drink as one wanted if friends or relations provided the money.

In the Felons' section life was far more brutal. Assuming that the prisoner had the necessary money to avoid fetters, he then went to the underground chambers where the criminal prisoners were kept. As soon as he appeared there were shouts of "Pay or strip!" and the money thus demanded was known as "chummage".

If the prisoner, as was usual, had no money and in addition was not strong enough to knock anyone down who approached him, he was normally stripped naked, his clothes sold to the gaolers, and he was then thrashed just as an example to the other newcomers. The criminal in the Felons' section of Newgate had very little chance of survival for long unless he had some source of money. The food which was officially provided was not handed out individually, but simply thrust into the room according to the number of prisoners there. Naturally the strongest grabbed the most.

If, however, the felon had plenty of money, life was at least by comparison bearable. He could go to the central drinking room where refreshments were obtainable at 4d. a quartern for brandy and 2s. a bottle for wine. The barman was also the salesman for candles which, as there were no windows in these underground cellars, were essential. For a fee of 1s. 6d. it was possible to spend a few minutes in an interview room where the prisoner could talk to his relatives and make arrangements to get more money. Beds cost 3s. 6d. a week, and without paying that fee a criminal simply slept on the floor. He was also expected to pay 14s. as an entrance fee even to be permitted to purchase privileges and to pay 1s. 6d. a week as his share for coals for heating and cooking and 1s. for what were dubiously called " Prisoners' Comforts ".

Not the least horrible sight of the Felons' section of Newgate up to the eighteenth century was the rooms nearby. The prisoners could, for example, see into what was known as the Hangman's Kitchen, where those executed for treason were brought and, after decapitation, the heads were boiled in herbs and salt so as to prevent decomposition or attacks by birds when the skulls were exposed in the city. Nearby also was the infamous Press Room.

Although there were small rooms for women prisoners in Newgate it was possible for both felons and debtors of both sexes to mix in the drinking rooms, and as a result immorality was rife throughout the prison. Scores of babies were born there and it was normal for prostitutes to pay fees to the gaolers to get inside Newgate at night.

One last section of Newgate requires to be mentioned. This was known as the Castle. It was set aside for prisoners of State and wealthy felons. Accommodation in these rooms cost anything from £20 to £500 plus the comparatively modest fee of 11s. 6d. a week for coals and candles.

Washing facilities in the prison were rudimentary, the main source being a single pump. Even by the low standards of hygiene of the prisoners, there were times when one of the inmates became so filthy that his companions would take him into the yard, strip him, and hold him under the pump for several minutes. Sanitation was even more rudimentary, and because of the large number of prisoners who were either imbecile or actually mad (at that time there was no such thing as a criminal lunatic) the physical state of the inmates and the rooms where they lived and slept can be conjectured.

Typhus fever was endemic in Newgate, and on occasions the deaths from the disease became so numerous that they caused a major scandal even in those easy-going days. In 1750 fever raged with such intensity that fifty of the officials of the Sessions House, ranging from the Lord Mayor to ushers, caught it. This disaster was the origin of spreading aromatic herbs and spraying vinegar around the court rooms to kill the smell. At that time, of course, it was not realised that typhus fever was spread by lice, and the belief was that its victims succumbed from the odours.

The custom of protection against the prison miasma is still observed by a token gesture today. It was one of my jobs to see that from May to September pot-pourri consisting of mint and camomile were placed in small heaps in the Courts of the Old Bailey on the first two days at the beginning of each Session. The Judges and officials of the Corporation of the City of London used to be given small bouquets of sweet-smelling flowers on these occasions.

The conditions of Newgate became so frightful that in 1770 a new building was begun and paid for out of the duty payable on the imports of coal into London. The original cost was estimated to be £50,000, but in actual fact the bill came to far more than this. Hardly had the building been completed than it was broken open during the Gordon riots of 1780 and set on fire. Scores of prisoners were liberated. Reconstruction cost a further £30,000.

Three years after the Gordon riots the work of Newgate Gaol increased still more because Tyburn ceased to be a place of execution. Over six centuries about 50,000 people had been hanged on the notorious gibbet which stood north-west of the present Marble Arch.

The Newgate executions were carried out publicly until 1868. The hangings were one of the sights of London and a good seat on the first floor of one of the public houses on the opposite side of the Old Bailey cost as much as fifty guineas.

The Governor of the prison used to give hanging breakfasts at which distinguished personages met for a large meal timed so that they ate while watching the unfortunate victim swing from the gibbet. It was certainly as well to be a friend of the Governor or to have the money for a seat in one of the houses around the Old Bailey, because the crowds in the street were always tremendous. In 1807, for example, twenty-eight people were killed by being crushed to death. Many hundreds were injured and the Out-Patients Department of nearby St. Bartholomew's Hospital was like a shambles.

But reform was in the air. The revelations of what conditions were like within Newgate, given by such people as Mrs. Elizabeth Fry, roused the conscience of all decent people. In a description of what she saw in the women's section of the prison in 1813, which horrified the nation, she told of crowds of half-naked women, many with babies in their arms, holding out wooden spoons on long sticks which they were able to poke through the grills of the windows in their cells, so as to beg for alms for food. Many of the women were dead drunk, and as many others were obviously insane. All whom Elizabeth Fry saw were wearing heavy leg irons riveted at the knees and ankles.

Despite the misgivings of the Governor and his insistence that these women were beyond redemption, she begged that the chains which linked each of the women to the next prisoner, so that when one fell she was simply dragged across the floor by the others, should be struck off and that she should be permitted to start a school for both the mothers and the children. She also managed to get female gaolers in place of the men.

By the time an Act was passed which made the Criminal Court of the City of London the Central Criminal Court, the savagery of legal punishment was easing. Only a few years before there were no fewer than two hundred offences punished by death and even little children were treated in the same way as the most hardened criminal. There is, for example, in the Old Bailey archives a record of a boy of nine years of age who was sentenced to be hanged for stealing goods to the value of 2d. from a shop window.

In 1830 the last known case of a man being placed in the pillory outside Newgate Prison occurred. A few years later it was removed. For thirty-four years after the establishment of the Court as we know it today, executions were carried out in public, providing a salacious entertainment for the London mob.

The last man to be hanged in front of Newgate was Michael Barrett, a Fenian, in 1868. Newgate ceased to be a prison in 1881, although executions still took place within the walls until 1902, a few weeks before the first hammer blow crashed on the heavy brick wall as demolition began.

The workman who gave that blow probably did not know that he fulfilled an ancient prophecy which is contained in the Old Bailey records—" an innocent man will one day break through the walls of Newgate ".

And so a few weeks before I joined the staff the new building was opened by King Edward VII.

There are a number of interesting facts about this famous building which has become such a notable feature of the skyline of the City. The whole structure is actually floating on the London clay, supported by an immense concrete raft which in places is twelve feet thick. The bronze figure of Justice which, I believe, is the only one in which the figure is not blindfolded, is about twenty feet high. It is just two hundred feet above the ground.

The Grand Hall, from which the forecourts open, stands underneath the great dome which is decorated with allegorical figures and is flanked on either side by two smaller domes.

The forecourts open directly from the first floor hall and on this floor are rooms for the witnesses immediately wanted and the offices for various officials, besides juries' and Judges' private rooms. The loggia opening off the corridor at the rear of the benches and at the far end communicating directly with a private entrance and staircase is the Lord Mayor's parlour, ante-room and the Aldermen's robing room.

The cells, which always seem to arouse the curiosity of the visitor, are quite separate from the Courts. The prison

vans arrive in a courtyard on the Ludgate Hill side where
prisoners are set down immediately outside the entrance
to the cells situated on the lower floors. Originally these
were eighteen in number and included eight sleeping cells
in case it might be necessary to keep a prisoner overnight
on account of sickness or for some other reason, but some
of these have now been changed into consultation rooms
and offices for the warders. There is no communication
between the cells and the other parts of the building except
by the staircases which lead to the dock.

The Courts, six in number, are awe-inspiring, more
because of the atmosphere produced by the dramas which
have been played out there than on account of their appearance. They are quite small and plain. In the centre of the
court room there is the dock—a small square which is
enclosed in panelling about four feet high. Steps lead into
it directly from the cells below. The public gallery in the
Courts accommodates about thirty people and the Bench,
considering the size of its chairs which are so heavy that
they move on rails, is really quite surprisingly small. The
jury box has comfortably upholstered seats bearing the
arms of the City. Witnesses and others concerned in the
case have an extremely small place allocated to them at the
rear of the dock.

Considering the size of the Old Bailey and the fact that
the immediately surrounding area was partially devastated
in the war, it is remarkable how little damage the Central
Criminal Court suffered from air raids. It was bombed
on the night of May 10-11, 1941, during the great fire blitz
on the City, and two of my colleagues who were fire-
watching at the time were killed. The bomb completely
destroyed Court No. 2. Repairs and reconstruction were
not finished until 1952 when the north-west corner of the
building was formally re-opened by the Lord Mayor. And
so it was that German bombs could not really affect the
existence of this famous and ancient Court of Justice.
While it has preserved intact its ancient ceremonial and
privileges it has advanced to keep pace with the immense

changes that have occurred during the onward march of modern civilisation, so that the entire spirit and method of administering justice now bears little relation to that of the cruel and intolerant years of the Court's infancy. Today the Old Bailey stands in the forefront of the institutions concerned with the protection of life, property and the wellbeing of the people.

It always surprises me, when I find that friends and acquaintances have very little idea of just what it is like inside one of the Courts of the Old Bailey. Of course, it is a basic principle of British justice that all trials must take place in a Court to which the public is admitted. But, at the same time, every effort is made today to get rid of any suggestion that it is some sort of show where ghouls may feast their eyes on some unfortunate person being condemned to death or sent away for many years' imprisonment.

Gone are the days which I knew when I first joined the staff of the Central Criminal Court when artists were sent by newspapers and magazines so that they could make vivid sketches of the Court during the most dramatic moment of trial, and today no one would dare, as happened during the trial of Crippen, to smuggle a camera inside.

To some extent the architects of the present building deliberately carried out designs with the object of preventing the Courts becoming a place of public curiosity and possibly entertainment. This applies in particular to Court No. 1, where, of course, most murders and other sensational trials take place.

The City of London authorities knew that under that old procedure, by tipping the attendants it was possible to get into the main part of the Court while similar gratuities resulted in the public gallery, directly above the dock, often being crammed with at least one hundred people.

The Committee of the Bar Mess agreed with the Corporation the accommodation for those people who had no direct interest in the case should be kept to a minimum. There are now two entrances from the hall which are guarded by City of London police who will normally allow entrance to everyone with a reasonable explanation, but certainly will not authorise mere sightseers to go any further. If the case is of any major public interest then the Sheriffs normally issue tickets which are obtainable only if the applicant can give a very good reason for wishing to be there.

The public gallery is, of course, open to anyone and is approached from a separate entrance in the street and up a flight of stairs. On almost every day a small queue can be seen waiting patiently to enter and some of the people in it apparently have nothing else with which to occupy their time, for they are well-known to the court attendants and appear day after day several hundred times a year. I very much doubt whether they have as vivid an impression of a trial as that obtained by the readers of the newspapers when a brilliant journalist creates a pen-picture of the scene.

The front row of the public gallery accommodates ten or twelve people and they have a fairly good view of the Court, although it is rather difficult for them to hear. Those who have to go in the rows behind can certainly see very little and unless they have very good hearing can hardly follow the case.

The restricted accommodation in the public gallery can sometimes have amusing results. Mr. Justice Humphreys was the presiding judge when some Sinn Feiners were due to be tried. Threatening messages were sent to the Court and to the City of London police that if the trial took place there might be some unfortunate incidents. Those which threatened the life of the Judge were regarded with great seriousness by the Commissioner of Police of the City of London, and he suggested to the Judge that the public gallery should be closed. He refused to permit this because of his desire to show that justice would be administered without fear or favour, and the matter of ensuring that the Judge's life was not in jeopardy was left to the police.

When the trial opened on the next day, the front row of the public gallery was occupied by a bunch of toughs, some almost in rags and all badly needing a shave and a bath. These gentlemen had arrived at an extremely early hour at the public entrance to the Court and they were first in the queue and so occupied the entire front row which was the only one from which a proper view of the Judge could be had.

They were, as a matter of fact, members of a police football team chosen for their brawn and bulk and had been told that for the duration of the trial they could wear the shabbiest clothes they liked and enjoy themselves listening to the administration of justice instead of safeguarding it on patrol.

Now let me describe the famous Court No. 1, as I have seen it over so many years. Dominating the scene is the judicial bench. There are six chairs, each so heavy that they run on rails. On the left hand side, as you face the Court, the first is occupied by the Judge's clerk, the next one is the seat of the High Court or presiding Judge. The centre seat is that always available for the Lord Mayor of London and it is above this seat that the Sword of Justice is fixed, it always being in the Court presided over by the Senior Judge. To the right of the Lord Mayor's seat is that for an Alderman and the last two for a Sheriff and Under-Sheriff of the City of London.

The Lord Mayor, Alderman and Sheriffs need not attend any Court throughout the whole trial, but they are present at its opening and an Alderman must be available within the building while a Court is sitting.

This section of the Court is, of course, raised on a dais and immediately below it, in front of the Judge's seat, is accommodation for the Clerk of the Court and the Court Usher. Beyond this section and between it and the witness box is the seat for the verbatim shorthand writer.

From all these positions the occupants look across the well of the Court to the focal point during the trial—the dock, which is quite large as it has to accommodate one or more prisoners and their warders, of whom there are normally two present for each prisoner.

The jury sit in two rows on the left of the prisoner as he faces the Judge and below the jury box are the seats for the newspaper reporters and for the police officer who represents the district in which the crime occurred. This officer's duty, by the way, is merely to watch over the interests of the police taking part in the trial. He has normally no actual part to play in the proceedings which are left to the police officers actually in charge of the case. These men sit at a large table immediately in front of the Press seats.

Beyond this table, and a little to the right hand side of the prisoner, but near enough so that he can readily communicate with him if he desires, is the accommodation for the Counsel for the Defence. To the right of the Defence's accommodation is that for the Counsel for the Prosecution.

To most people the principal actors in the drama of a criminal trial are the Judge, counsel, witnesses and prisoner. A visitor to the Court will usually be surprised at the important role played by the man in wig and gown, who is extremely busy at the outset of the proceedings. From the fact that he sits down immediately below the Judge we know that it is the Clerk of the Court, who, by the way, is also known as the Clerk of the Peace. He is the man who has made all the arrangements for the trial. It is he who draws the indictment. This is a printed statement of the offence for which the prisoner is charged and it has to be prepared with the utmost care or the case may well be null and void.

The Clerk also sees to the depositions, which are notes of the evidence taken in the lower Court at which it was decided that the case should go to the Old Bailey. He sees that they are copied and made available to the Judge and counsel.

Normally the Clerk of the Court selects the Counsel for the Defence because, in the majority of murder cases—for some strange reason it is quite rare for a wealthy person to commit murder—the prisoner is granted Legal Aid and the State pays the cost of the defence, so that the Clerk of the Court has to choose a counsel to defend the prisoner from a panel of Queen's Counsel and Junior Counsel which is maintained at the Old Bailey. The fees paid even in the most notorious trials of today are very modest indeed and the days when enormous sums were paid to famous counsel are certainly in the past.

Many people believe that a murder trial is an extremely costly business, but ignoring the routine overheads of Judge's salary and so on, the charge accruing from the legal services for the prosecution and the defence can be very small indeed.

It is unusual for a murderer to insist on pleading guilty, but when he does (and I recall a case shortly after the war) the total sum involved did not exceed over £40. Even in prolonged cases where witnesses are brought from long distances, and there may be experts who give evidence for more than one day, the costs for a modern trial are only about £2,000.

But the real worth of the Old Bailey is not to be expressed in terms of money. Its supremacy as a Court of Law, protecting the innocent and inflicting just penalties on the guilty, is something of priceless value to London and the nation.

CHAPTER TWO

Infamous Old Bailey Criminals

IN THAT REMARKABLE PUBLICATION WHICH records the worst of the criminals who have appeared in the Old Bailey, " The Hangman's Record ", there are the names of hundreds of men and women who went to the gallows in the past four hundred years after trial at the Old Bailey. Many of them were crude killers whose story is of little importance, but here and there is a name which has remained in history.

On May 22, 1701, for instance, it records the execution of Captain James Kidd for piracy. This was one of the most remarkable trials during a century notable for notorious criminals. Kidd and nine of his fellow pirates were brought to trial at the Old Bailey on May 8. Offences committed on the high seas were, at that time, under the jurisdiction of the Court of Admiralty and there was a section of the Old Bailey's administration known as the Admiralty Sessions, its difference from that of the ordinary Sessions being that the Judge of the Court of Admiralty presided and charged the Grand Jury.

A true bill was returned against Kidd for murder and piracy, and against the other prisoners for piracy. Dr. Oxenden was the Admiralty Judge and he was assisted by the Lord Chief Justice Baron Ward and four other judges, indicating that this was a case of unusual importance.

Kidd's alleged crime was all the more reprehensible because he had originally been sent out to catch pirates. A native of Greenwich, he had during the wars with France commanded a privateer, sailing with his ship in company with units of the English Navy and swooping on French privateers and French naval vessels in the Caribbean.

Afterwards he settled in the colony of New York and began a commercial enterprise trading by coaster down the

25

Atlantic sea-board of North America. The number of pirates infesting these waters was so large that when Kidd suggested that he could easily tackle the problem the Governor of Massachusetts Bay officially appointed him as a sort of coastguard. Only because the Admiralty in London were short of ships was his proposal that he should be given a commission in the Royal Navy and actually command a man-of-war for the job turned down. Kidd was, however, presented by Whitehall with a special commission under the Great Seal of England. Some of the principal Officers of State, including the Lord High Chancellor and the First Lord of the Admiralty, financed the enterprise.

His ship, named the *Adventure,* sailed from Plymouth on May 1, 1696, with a crew of eighty. Before she had crossed the Atlantic Kidd had captured one French ship. Then for three years there was no authentic news of what he was doing, but a number of powers friendly to the United Kingdom began protesting that their vessels were being chased by a ship whose description closely tallied with that of the *Adventure.*

Kidd heard of the international protests that were being made, and realised the game was nearly up. He got rid of the enormous booty that he had taken during this period from innumerable ships all along the Atlantic seaboard of America and as far east as Madagascar, by hiding the bulk of his treasure on Gardner's Island where, incidentally, it is believed it still remains.

Kidd then put in at Boston, where much to his indignation he was arrested and sent to London for trial.

Important legal considerations were involved because of the fact that high Officers of State were identified with the enterprise and it could be shown that Kidd had been officially given very wide facilities to do what he thought best in order to clear the seas of hostile ships.

Kidd was taken before the Bar of the House of Commons in order to allow him the chance of showing that members of the Government were personally involved. The pirate arrived there half-drunk, but he would not admit that he had ever indulged in illegal acts on the high seas and it was to his credit that he never said one word implicating the men who had financed his activities.

At the subsequent Old Bailey trial he pleaded not guilty to the very serious charge of piracy and the authorities were only too eager to concentrate on the charge of murder. Compared with the more serious accusation murder of a member of his crew was comparatively a minor matter.

It was alleged that in October 1697 Kidd had struck his gunner on the head with a bucket and smashed his skull in. Kidd's defence took the line that the man was fomenting mutiny concerned with his proposal to the crew to attack a Dutch merchantman. Unfortunately the other members of the crew gave a different version of the incident which indicated that Kidd had attacked the man in a frenzy of temper. The jury convicted him.

Even though this meant that Kidd's life was forfeited the trial on the charge of piracy then proceeded. The evidence revealed a fantastic tale of barbaric cruelty, and an acquisition of loot from victims on the seven seas of the world, the value of which was virtually incalculable.

Kidd's defence was that he had been given authority to attack and capture French privateers and to the best of his knowledge all the ships with which he had engaged were either French or sailing with French passes. As the ships he had captured, looted and destroyed belonged to almost every seafaring nation in the world, there was little likelihood of either Judge or jury accepting this excuse, and inevitably Kidd was convicted on this charge as well.

As he listened to the sentence of death (which was also pronounced on several of his fellow pirates) Kidd shouted out: " It is a very hard sentence. I am the innocentest person of them all, only I have been sworn against by perjured persons."

He was not hanged at Newgate Prison but, as was always the case with pirates, he was taken to Execution Dock and hanged just above low tide mark in the sight of all vessels using the Port of London.

In May 1725 the records show a particularly busy time. On one day, May 24, no fewer than nine men were executed at Tyburn for robbery and murder. They were members of a desperate gang and their leader, the infamous Jonathan Wild, was among them. Without doubt Wild was the worst gangster who has ever disgraced the name of London, and although at the time he was given the title of the Prince of Robbers, he was in reality a vicious and faithless man beside whom even the major crooks of today pale into insignificance.

Wild was born in Wolverhampton and came to London to work for a buckle maker. He soon fell into debt and as a result was imprisoned. He seemed even at that time to have plentiful sources of income and he was able to pay the necessary bribes to the gaolers so as to gain the privileges thereby obtainable. In some way he managed to gain the job of assisting the gaoler by accepting prisoners brought in by the night watchman, and helping to escort them into Court on the following morning.

Wild was in prison for some months, and as a result he got to know personally hundreds of petty criminals and when he was released he immediately started up in business as a gangster.

Before very long he had an organisation of pickpockets, foot-pads, robbers and highwaymen which eliminated the competition and quarrelling which had previously prevailed, so that these crooks worked in strict co-operation and on a definite plan of strategy.

Scores of children were used as messengers between perpetrators of crimes and Wild, so that he very quickly obtained knowledge of the identity of the victim and a description of the goods which had been stolen. Thereupon Wild wrote a letter to the victim, or if he was important enough, called upon him, explaining that by pure chance a dealer friend of his had come into possession of some valuables which he believed belonged to the person concerned.

Wild went on to say that the dealer was an honest man and while he had no desire to traffic in stolen goods it was only reasonable that he should be recompensed for the money he had expended, and his conscience eased with a promise from the victim that no action should be taken to try and catch the criminal who had brought the goods for sale. As the dupe knew only too well that the police force of the time was so inefficient that any possibility of it retrieving the goods was remote, he usually agreed to this arrangement as the lesser of two evils.

Wild's uncanny ability to locate stolen goods became so well known that victims began to approach him before he got in touch with them and as a result his premises in Cock Alley, Cripplegate, became a sort of stolen property office where clients paid a 5s. registration fee so that full details of their loss could be entered in his books. When these visitors told Wild of a robbery about which he knew nothing, his minions soon discovered who the independent crook was and he was told that it would be safer for his skin to hand his loot over. Wild quickly became very rich and in 1715 he purchased a luxurious house in the Old Bailey itself, from which he would sally forth each morning, carrying a decorated staff intended to suggest that it was some official symbol of his office.

For ten years nobody seemed to be able to do anything, but at length he was caught red-handed attempting to assist a smuggler to escape the law. Then one or two courageous citizens who ignored the threats of violence and even death which members of Wild's so-called Corporation of Thieves made, came forward with evidence of his complicity in the robberies from which they had suffered.

During his trial at the Old Bailey evidence was given that he had divided London into zones, each with its own staff of criminals, and there were full details of the strict regulations which he imposed which prevented the crooks of one trespassing on the area of another. Down on the Thames embankment there were huge warehouses crammed with the stolen goods he had obtained, and so vast were his supplies that he actually bought two ships which made regular sailings to the Netherlands in order to get rid of the surplus, returning with contraband spirits.

Even with all this damning evidence, Wild's conviction was by no means certain. He had always been careful to employ only convicted thieves in his Corporation, and at that time the evidence of a felon was regarded as worthless. In such cases where his employees appeared to him to be in possession of knowledge that might result in his conviction he had framed them so that they had either been transported or executed. During the trial he actually handed the jury a list of sixty-seven people who had been hanged because of his evidence to the authorities.

The last few days of his life were as spectacular as his criminal career. In prison, he declined to attend any religious service by pretending he was feeling unwell, but he insisted on the other prisoners keeping order in the cells, and on the day that he was due to be executed he agreed to receive Communion. On the way from the chapel he swallowed some laudanum in an attempt to cheat the gallows, but he took such a large dose that he vomited it up and thus defeated his object.

When the cart arrived to convey him to Tyburn he was still semi-conscious from the effects of the drug, and he was oblivious to the yells of the mob and showers of filth which were hurled at him all along the road. As he was in no condition to stand up while the noose was placed about his neck, the hangman left him to recover further while he busied himself with the other eight rogues who were to be executed that morning.

This delay made the mob suspect that Wild had arranged some scheme to cheat the gallows and they became so menacing to the executioner that he immediately made arrangements for Wild's death, who was still in a semi-coma.

Wild was buried, as he had requested, alongside Betty

Mann, one of the women with whom he had lived, in St. Pancras Churchyard. A few mornings later a grave-digger saw that during the night the grave had been disturbed and the body stolen.

The Tyburn mob's suspicions about the hangman's tardiness in dealing with Wild were not without foundation. Until comparatively recent times the method of execution did not allow for a long drop in order to break the neck. The victims were, in fact, slowly strangled. By chance or through deliberate action this meant that surprisingly often convicted felons were able to cheat the gallows.

In 1705, for example, a thief named John Smith was tried at the Old Bailey and duly taken for execution at Tyburn. He was suspended for the time which the law ordained, but his friends restored him to life when they got hold of the body. Foolishly, he soon committed another crime and was back in Newgate Prison where he died on the day prior to his trial.

Three years after Wild was hanged, there was the famous case of Margaret Dickson, who was sentenced to be hanged for infanticide. This case occurred in Scotland and after she had been suspended for the usual time her body was cut down and was being conveyed in a coffin by cart towards Musselburgh. The driver of the cart went to a tavern for a drink and while he was there the corpse pushed away the lid of the coffin, got out, and entered the tavern— to the considerable dismay of the driver! The happy ending to this story was that Margaret was able to prove beyond all doubt that she had been innocent of the killing of her child.

How many people cheated the gallows through the help of influential friends will never be known as it was obviously to their advantage to keep the matter secret, but in November 1740 a group of surgeons, one of them Sir William Petty, obtained the bodies of two criminals, a man and a woman, for dissection. The woman was Eleanor Munoman and she showed signs of life when the dissecting knife was applied to her three hours after she had been cut down from the scaffold. The doctors then carefully examined the man, William Duell, who had been convicted of murder, and resuscitated him. Duell was transported for life, but it was thought that the woman had suffered enough. She was set free, eventually married and lived happily as a wife and mother.

The agony of slow death by strangulation sometimes had a different result of creating frantic hopes that they might be able to survive. In 1760 Earl Ferrers, who was convicted of the murder of his steward, was believed to be the first man who paid a fee to the hangman so that there was considerable slack in the rope while the guard supported his feet, the result being that when he moved away the jerk would effectively break the victim's neck.

The noble earl, although so anxious to die quickly, thoroughly enjoyed his last hours on earth. He drove in his own carriage from Newgate to Tyburn bowing and waving to the crowds. He was hanged with a rope which he had himself ordered. It was made of silk.

The end of the eighteenth century marked the beginning of more humane conception of punishment for crime. The Bow Street Runners were enforcing law and order in a large area of London, and Tyburn's ghastly record was closing. Years were to pass before the modern conception of justice softened the harsh practices of the Old Bailey and of Newgate, but the day of the unprincipled enemy of society who, whatever his crime, knew that his life was forfeit if he was caught, was over.

CHAPTER THREE

"Not Guilty!"

SIX MONTHS AFTER I JOINED THE STAFF of the Old Bailey there occurred what expert criminologists have described as the classic unsolved murder mystery of the twentieth century. It was of absorbing interest to me as the first of the notorious and spectacular trials that I have ever watched.

The "Rising Sun" murder trial was historic, too. It was the first occasion in an English Court that a person accused of murder, giving evidence on his own behalf as permitted by the Criminal Evidence Act of 1898, successfully defended his innocence. For Robert Wood was proven "not guilty".

The trial had been set for November 1907, but had to be postponed owing to delays at the Police Court hearing. This helped to arouse public interest to fever-heat by the time the Old Bailey case began a month afterwards.

Mr. Justice Grantham was the judge, but such was the judicial interest in the case that it was common to see most of the other judges at the Central Criminal Court dropping in to listen. Crown Counsel were led by Sir Charles Mathews and the defence was in the hands of the great Sir Edward Marshall Hall, who early set the tone of excitement of the whole trial by the comparatively unusual procedure of challenging two jurors, who were dismissed.

The public section of the Court was packed with notabilities. Sir Hall Caine, then at the zenith of his fame as a novelist, was there, and other writers who came to learn at first hand that truth can indeed be stranger than fiction included A. E. W. Mason and Sir Arthur Pinero. George R. Sims came on the first day, and I recall meeting Oscar Asche, H. B. Irving and Seymour Hicks—actors who were to me the remote figures beyond the footlights. But now

2

they were the audience—watching real life drama in which the leading player had indeed to give the performance of his life.

Robert Wood was an artist, the son of a Scotsman who had long lived in London. After a short period as a steward in an Australian medical students' club in Chancery Lane he had worked his way up to a senior position with a firm of glassware manufacturers in Gray's Inn Road. Some of the most beautiful cut glass on sale in London at that time carried Wood's designs.

His behaviour in Court was uncannily serene. Throughout the five long days of the hearing he listened with interest but perfect calmness to the ominously damning circumstantial evidence. He heard details of the secretive and immoral side of his life revealed with relentless insistence. Yet he seemed to regard the entire trial with more objective attention than any of the gaping members of the public in the Court. He passed the time making life-like sketches of the court room, the Judge, and the faces of the witnesses and legal personalities. A few of my colleagues managed to secure some of the sketches as souvenirs, and those that I saw were perfect cameos, reviving in my mind exactly the impression of character as well as appearance of the person concerned.

The murder of which Robert Wood was accused revealed something of the night life of an ostensibly conventional section of middle class London society at that time, and the picture that was drawn with such care and in such detail during that memorable trial was not a pretty one.

The sordid tragedy began on the morning of September 11, 1907, when a railway train chef named Shaw got ready to leave his home in St. Paul's Road, Camden Town. He was living there with a woman the neighbours thought was Mrs. Phyllis Shaw, but who was, in fact, Emily Dimmock.

Shaw worked on the Scottish expresses, travelling between London and Sheffield, going down on the afternoon train and returning on the early morning train the next day. Thus he was away from home for roughly twenty-four hours and then had twenty-four hours off.

The routine meant that Phyllis was left on her own to a great extent. Shaw was aware that before she came to live with him she had pursued an immoral life, but whether he really believed that she had entirely abandoned it as she had promised to do, was doubtful. She did at least conceal her activities from him as much as she could.

Phyllis remained in bed until the afternoon after her husband had left. Then she got up, put on a lot of make-up, dressed herself in her second-best clothes, forgot to take the curling pins out of her hair, and went to what at that time was a tawdrily gay part of London—the Euston Road and Tottenham Court Road area. The scores of public houses in the district provided a cheap version of the glittering West End of the Edwardian era. They were infested by women of the town and visited by clerks and provincial business men out for an inexpensive good time where they could " see life ".

In the early evening Phyllis made the rounds of the public houses, including her favourite, " The Rising Sun ". On the previous three nights she had met a ship's cook there and on at least one of the nights had taken him home with her. But on this particular night he did not meet her, as he was later able to prove in Court with a cast-iron alibi—a fact which did not worry Phyllis, who, as the barmaid observed, was clearly expecting somebody else.

The meeting she had planned presumably took place, for Phyllis was not in the saloon bar when closing time approached. She was on the way to her Camden Town home with her companion—and before dawn this companion had killed her, slashing at her neck with such force that the head remained attached to the body only by some half-severed muscles.

It was thus that Shaw found her at midday when he smashed through the locked bedroom door, his forebodings aroused when she failed to answer him and because the living room was in utter confusion, the contents of drawers and cupboards scattered all over the floor.

Phyllis was lying face downwards and naked under the bedclothes. The blood from the wound had soaked through the mattress and had formed a pool near the fireplace. Despite the frightful nature of the attack on her the position of the body and the undisturbed bedclothes indicated that she had died so suddenly that there could have been hardly any struggle. Clearly whoever had struck with such sub-human force had done so without warning and had been able to approach her without arousing any suspicion of the terrible scheme seething in his brain.

The police rapidly reconstructed the last twenty-four hours of the victim's life. The evidence of two dirty plates and of the post-mortem on her stomach indicated that she had taken a meal in the kitchen with some companion about midnight. Publicans, barmaids and revellers were able to provide a reasonably detailed account of her activities until 11 p.m., and in particular they could describe a man who had been seen with her both on the fatal night and on previous occasions.

In the official description issued by the authorities he was " about thirty years of age, 5ft. 8ins. in height. He has a long thin blotchy face and sunken eyes. He was wearing a blue serge suit, a bowler hat with a somewhat high crown, a double collar and a dark tie. He is a man of good education and of shabby genteel appearance."

Within a matter of hours this description was amplified by dramatic evidence. An unemployed man who had risen early to go in search of a job had been walking down St. Paul's Road shortly before 5 a.m. The street was deserted at that hour, and the lamps in the adjoining goods yard were going out as the first rays of dawn stole across the shabby houses. A noise behind him made him turn. He saw a man with a peculiar jerkiness in his walk leave Shaw's house, turn in the opposite direction, and with overcoat collar up and his bowler hat well down over his face, hurry away.

That this was the murderer there could be little doubt. The police surgeon's estimate of the time of the attack was about 4 a.m.

The investigation was intensified. The ransacking of the rooms suggested that the assailant had feverishly searched for some incriminating evidence, for there were no valuables in the place and in any event nothing of monetary value appeared to be missing.

It was at first thought that he must have found what he was looking for, generally regarded by the detectives as a postcard which it was known Phyllis had received the previous morning. But chance favoured the police. While Shaw was tidying up he moved the lining paper in one of the drawers. Underneath he found a postcard. The picture was of a woman holding a child. On the other side was Phyllis's name and address plus a brief message written in indelible pencil. It said: " Phyllis darling. If it pleases you, meet me 8.15pm at the —— " a semi-circle with strokes radiating from the circumference had been cleverly sketched in at this point—" yours to a cinder, Alice."

Experts who examined the card gave their opinion that the writing was a man's. The signature of "Alice " was obviously a way of allaying Shaw's suspicions if he happened to see the missive.

I well remember the nation-wide excitement on the morning of September 29, a Sunday, when newspaper posters reproduced the writing and sketch, and further reproductions were printed in the papers, demanding of millions if they recognised the writing and offering a reward for information.

The result of the publication of this message with its drawing of " The Rising Sun " was not known to the police for some time, but the evidence at the trial indicated how effective Press publicity can be in a hunt for a criminal.

A girl named Ruby Young read a newspaper as she lay in bed that Sunday morning, thought she recognised the writing—she certainly knew the victim—and started to write a letter to the Editor claiming the reward for the information she set down. But she had no stamp and was too lazy to get up till the evening. By that time there was a knock on the door of her flat in Earl's Court and she found the man whom she suspected standing there.

He was Robert Wood, a friend of hers. He admitted that he was in trouble and began explaining how he had come to write the card. According to his story, he had been in " The Rising Sun " when a hawker came in selling postcards. A woman he had heard some men calling Phyllis turned to him and asked his opinion about one of the cards, explaining that she collected them. Wood said that he considered the hawker's stock vulgar and nasty, and on the spur of the moment offered her an artistic production he happened to have in his pocket. The girl thanked him and asked him to write something on the card as a souvenir, posting it afterwards to her address, which she gave.

Wood went on to say that he thought it would be flattering to her if he made his message sound like an invitation to a meeting at the pub in which they were sitting. He then put the card in his pocket, forgot to post it—and by chance ran into Phyllis the next day, who told him how disappointed she had been not to get the card. He posted it shortly afterwards. Still another chance meeting occurred ; he saw Phyllis in " The Rising Sun " the next evening. She was talking to a lame man to whom she said, as he prepared to leave, " See you later ".

That was Wood's story to Ruby Young. She was impressed sufficiently not to post her application for the newspaper reward.

To a foreman at Wood's glass works who also recognised the writing the young man gave a similar explanation, adding in this instance that his aged and invalid father would be deeply upset if he knew that his son was indulging in drink and the companionship of street women in his spare time. This man also agreed to keep quiet.

Wood might never have aroused the interest of the police if Ruby Young had managed to keep her secret to herself.

Womanlike, she had to tell somebody, and with insistent demands for complete confidence, she recounted all her conversation—plus some subsequent pleas on the part of Wood that she should say that he was always in her company on Mondays and Wednesdays—to a girl friend. The friend promptly confided in a lover, and as he was a newspaper reporter the secret was out. On the evening of October 4 a police inspector invited Wood to accompany him to Highgate police station.

At this stage it seemed that the killer of Phyllis Dimmock had been caught. But the evidence at the trial soon indicated that this was by no means the cut and dried case that superficially it appeared to be.

True, Wood had attempted to silence witnesses or to make them commit perjury. True, also, that he was something of a hypocrite in behaving in an exemplary manner at work and at home, while carousing in the most doubtful sort of company evening after evening. True indeed was it that he had written a postcard which suggested a meeting however much he protested it was all a joke.

But against this damning evidence were the irrefutable facts which immediately introduced strong doubts. Wood had not been at all secretive in his meeting with Phyllis in " The Rising Sun " and other taverns ; scores of people had seen him, and most agreed that it seemed a chance acquaintanceship on the vital evening, with no attempt by Wood to conceal his intentions. His effort to make Ruby Young say that he had been with her on the evening concerned was of no value in providing an alibi for a murder committed at four o'clock on the subsequent morning.

Wood's innocence, despite the appalling amount of circumstantial evidence, became more and more clear as the trial proceeded. The unemployed man had talked about seeing the stranger leaving the house of death in the lamplight, but it was proved that the lamps had been extinguished by then. He had spoken of the man wearing an overcoat. Wood had not worn an overcoat that night.

A neighbour of the Wood family had seen the young man enter the front door of his home about midnight, and his brother had heard him tiptoe into his father's room to borrow an alarm clock shortly afterwards.

The Judge in his summing up caused one of those rare storms of uncontrolled cheers when he said that in his opinion, despite the strong suspicions aroused, the prosecution had not brought the case home near enough to the accused.

This was also the jury's opinion. Wood had stood revealed as a liar, a hypocrite, an immoral playboy, but he was not a murderer.

The exciting scenes in the Court were followed by amazing incidents in Newgate Street and Holborn. Strong bodies of police forced a passage through the mass of laughing, cheering people who jammed the roadway solid and got Wood and his relatives into a teashop on the corner of Newgate Street. The crowd surged round and yelled for a speech. Wood did not come out, but his father came to a window and, with tears running down his face, tried to voice his thanks on behalf of his son and himself.

A crowd suffering from hysteria is a terrifying thing. The men, women and children who seemed so generous in their sympathy and kindness towards the defendant then turned into a baying, heartless monster as in some magical fashion the idea went through them all to seek out Ruby Young.

The middle and working classes who composed the crowd were in those days strait-laced and pitiless about feminine immorality. A girl of the class that Phyllis had represented was regarded as better dead, and even though Ruby was certainly no professional prostitute her lax morality with Wood over some years, as revealed in Court, classed her as little better. Although she had never claimed the newspaper reward of £100 and had never received it, the crowd seemed to think that this motive of greed was the reason why she had contrived Wood's arrest.

Police officers inside the Old Bailey were told by their

comrades outside that a plan was on foot to lynch her. The terrified girl, waiting to leave the building, was taken into a room where the cleaners kept their brooms and pails. There she changed into the clothes of a charwoman, and shadowed by two plain clothes policemen she left by the staff entrance, walking unrecognised through the crowd screaming for her blood as far as Ludgate Circus where she was put on a bus that took her into oblivion—the desirable goal which was also achieved by Robert Wood, who changed his name and place of employment soon afterwards.

The " Rising Sun " murder case was an example of an unfathomable mystery. My memory travels through nearly four decades for another example of drama where the climax came with the jury foreman's words " not guilty ".

The case I have in mind presented no mystery as to the identity of the only possible assailant—if there was any assailant at all, but offered a nice problem on the eternal question of " what exactly is murder? "

The case occurred during a serious phase of the Second World War and attracted but little attention in the national Press of the time because of the pressure of war news and the shortage of newsprint. If it had occurred in peacetime I feel sure that it would have been front page news with the public avidly discussing the evidence in this tragedy of love and jealousy.

The defendant was a splendid figure of a man—looking younger than the forty-three years of his age. His name was Ludomir Cienski and he was a distinguished officer in the Polish Army. The medals he wore at his trial were evidence enough of his bravery ; the fact that he had escaped to continue the fight against his country's oppressors in England was proof that he was a man of honour ; his dignified bearing in Court impressed everyone that, despite the terrible charge hanging over his head, he was no crude and brutal killer.

The story that led to his arrest was the all-too-common one—" one of the oldest stories in the world ", as his judge,

Mr. Justice Humphreys, described it—involving his wife's lover.

Lieutenant Cienski was working in the Polish Army headquarters in London and had a small flat near Victoria. His duties took him away from home quite often, and he noticed that his wife appeared cold and strange when he returned. After a few days her affection was renewed, but with the next absence from home the familiar feeling that something was wrong returned.

It did not take the worried husband very long to discover that the reason for her emotional crisis was her friendship with another officer, a Lieutenant Buchowski in the Polish Navy.

Cienski determined to thrash out the problem of their three loves by talking it over with his rival as man to man. Buchowski agreed to keep an appointment, and one morning they went into the sitting room, closed the door, and after a few minutes there were three gunshots.

The landlord heard the noise and rushed into the room. He stated in Court that he found Buchowski slumped in an armchair, dead. A yard or two away stood Cienski, the revolver in his hand.

When the police arrived Cienski gave a calm and coherent statement. " I tried to get him to promise not to see my wife again," he said. " He refused. I handed him my revolver and asked him to shoot me. If he shot me it did not matter. He fired at me. When he did so I jumped at him and caught the hand holding the revolver. There was a struggle. I heard shots. He fell back in the chair. I did not shoot him."

The detectives began an examination of the room and the body to see if this story was true. They had some doubts about it because the landlord had said that the three shots came in quick succession, while Cienski's story suggested that there should have been an interval between the first one and the other two.

The revolver had three empty chambers. There were two bullets in the body of the dead man and one had smashed into the wall opposite the chair where the corpse was lying. It seemed reasonable, therefore, to accept the story that Buchowski had fired in the direction of Cienski with the first bullet. The position of the gun when the other two were fired became vitally important, for it was not easy to accept that the man holding the gun had been so easily overcome that it was turned on himself.

One bullet, according to the evidence of Sir Bernard Spilsbury who was called in to make an examination, had penetrated the heart, killing him instantly, while the last shot had grazed the face—after death. This view was not quite so serious as it sounded—the circulation of the blood stops instantly when a bullet penetrates the heart and so a wound a moment later above the heart (on the face, for example) would not bleed—but it was serious enough, for it hardly tallied with Cienski's description of the tussle between two living men when all the shots were fired.

Against this ominous evidence, there was justification for the first part of his story. The husband was known to have threatened to shoot himself, and his wife's friend had written a letter in which he callously said: " For God's sake enough of these stories of the revolver. Leave him the magazine clip. Let him shoot himself, because one life is less important than three, or even two, ruined ones."

Lieutenant Cienski was inevitably charged with murder and in due course appeared at the Old Bailey, where Sir Patrick Hastings defended him.

As the case proceeded an amazing lapse on the part of the police was revealed. I think everyone was awaiting the police evidence of a scientific nature. A generation reared on crime film and detective fiction tends to place more faith in the evidence of fingerprints than is perhaps justified in real life. But in this case, where a man's life depended on the truth about who had held the weapon, it was obvious to all that the existence of the dead man's prints on the gun as well as those of Cienski would have gone a long way to confirm the defendant's story. By contrast, the absence of the dead man's prints would have virtually destroyed his chances.

Shamefacedly, the police officer had to admit that he did not know whether Buchowski's prints were on the gun or not. No tests for prints were ever made.

Sir Patrick Hastings after the trial described the Judge's summing up as a masterpiece. It was a supreme example of impartiality. Mr. Justice Humphreys stressed the fact that the prisoner was a foreigner, and for that reason a story that coming from the lips of an Englishman would have sounded fantastic might, if the jury understood the psychological background involved, be a reasonable version. If the story was unacceptable and the jury considered that the fatal shot—the second one—had been fired in a state of excitement and without the deliberate intention of killing it was open to return a verdict of manslaughter.

The jury was out for just under an hour. The defendant, back in the dock, awaited the verdict, impassive of face, splendid in his fatalistic calmness. I had the impression that his own conscience was clear whatever the citizens of the country he had adopted as his friend and ally might say.

There were no applause, no cheering, not even a murmur of excited discussion when the foreman clearly pronounced the two words that left Cienski a free man. Yet I believe that the sense of satisfaction that justice had really been done for the proud, emotionless and deeply wronged man in the dock was as profound among court officials, lawyers, and the handful of British and Polish people who had come to watch the trial as any at any time in the history of the Old Bailey.

CHAPTER FOUR

The Methods of the Poisoner

THE TWO MURDERS WHICH REMAIN MOST vividly in my mind concerned the use of poison. Ever since civilised man tackled the problem of crime and its punishment, the poisoner has been loathed more than any other kind of killer. In Rome the authorities inflicted a terrible form of punishment: the convicted murderer was compelled to die by his own weapon.

In this country Henry VIII created the law which demanded that poisoners should be boiled alive. Even since then a murderer convicted of poisoning has far less chance of experiencing the mercy of the Court than other types of killer. It is extremely rare for a poisoner to be reprieved.

I very much doubt whether we shall often read of any great and notorious poison case, for today the scientific ability to detect traces of poison is so efficient that if any would-be murderer is unwise enough to use this weapon the case will almost inevitably be solved.

But it was not always so, and in my early days at the Old Bailey it was cynically said that the number of trials on charges of poisoning were comparatively few for the simple reason that it was the most successful form of murder.

Until the great trials which I am going to recount took place there can be little doubt that a large number of poisoners remained undetected. A poisoning case, by the way, created the situation which resulted in a large number of crimes committed outside the London area being tried at the Old Bailey.

William Palmer, who has been given the dubious honour of the title of Prince of Poisoners, was arrested on charges of three murders, and it is fairly certain that he committed five others, mostly on members of his own family, for the sake of the insurance money.

Because of the local prejudice against him in his native county of Staffordshire—the crimes had been committed at Rugeley, where my mother was born—a law was passed in 1856 which enabled cases to be transferred from provincial assizes to the Central Criminal Court.

Some idea of the difficulties which doctors and scientists experienced in those days of analysing a poison can be gleaned from the fact that at Palmer's trial four experts gave evidence inferring that poison had been administered and twelve called for the defence refuted it. Palmer was found guilty, and although there can be no doubt that the poison he used was strychnine, its existence in the victims' bodies was never legally proved.

It is small wonder, in view of the ignorance of local doctors at that time about diseases and the symptoms of poisoning, that would-be murderers chose the poison weapon. Doctors filled in death certificates with vague details, which today would never be accepted by the authorities. The likelihood that, should the worst come to the worst, no proof of the existence of the poison in the victim's body would be forthcoming at the trial made the risk of punishment less than with other weapons.

The man whose name has become a by-word as a modern poisoner was the central figure in the dramatic trial in September 1910. His name was Dr. Hawley Harvey Crippen. He was the mildest and meekest little man I have ever seen in the dock at the Old Bailey on a major charge. At the time of his trial he was forty-eight years of age. It was quite clear that the four months' purgatory through which he had lived since he poisoned his wife at their home in Hilldrop Crescent, Camden Hill, had told severely on him. He looked older than his years and very ill. No one less like the master criminal of unsurpassed resources and cunning have I ever seen.

These were the days of long speeches by Counsel, and Mr. Richard Muir, who led for the Crown, spent a long time outlining the life of the prisoner with his gay but discontented wife, followed by the gradual blossoming of an illicit romance with Crippen's typist, Ethel le Neve. Then came the story of the finding of the remains of a body under the cellar floor at the house, Crippen's subsequent flight across the Atlantic with his mistress dressed as a boy, and the dramatic use of wireless telegraphy for the first time in the history of police investigation to effect Crippen's arrest. The account left little doubt in the mind of most people that the result of the trial was a foregone conclusion.

The basis of the defence was that Mrs. Crippen had run off with an unknown lover and that Dr. Crippen had made up some story about her visiting relatives in America in order to conceal the scandal.

The defence's explanation of the body in the cellar was that it had been put there by some previous tenant and it was, of course, the prosecution's task to prove that the remains were definitely those of Mrs. Crippen.

It was the medical evidence on this point that produced the greatest sensations of the trial. The task for the prosecution was extremely difficult, for Crippen, having excellent medical knowledge, had gone to fantastic lengths to ensure that identification of the remains was well-nigh impossible. The head and limbs were missing—and, as a matter of fact, were never discovered. One of the detectives, who had worked on the case, told me afterwards that it was believed Crippen had taken them in a suitcase and dumped them overboard during a holiday trip from Newhaven to Dieppe.

Every visible detail which indicated the sex of the corpse, as well as some of the internal organs, had been removed with great skill.

But Crippen had forgotten one tiny detail. The police in going into the previous life of Mrs. Crippen had been told by relatives that she had undergone an operation to remove the ovaries. The surgery involved in an ovariotomy involves only the slightest of visible marks. Crippen had ignored this mark and there was one tiny piece of flesh discovered which contained scar tissue.

This piece of flesh, together with a few others which could help in assessing the age and sex of the victim, produced a horrific spectacle in the Court. I watched eight famous surgeons and doctors who gave evidence on one side or the other peering at the tiny tragic remains of Mrs. Crippen as they were handed round the Court in a soup plate. The defence's suggestion was that the scar was, in reality, merely a fold in the skin caused after death.

It was to refute this theory that a tall and immaculately dressed young man, wearing a red carnation in his button-hole and answering Counsel's questions in a voice bereft of any emotion, but with tremendous confidence, started on his long career which was to make him easily the most famous forensic expert of the century. He was Dr. Bernard Spilsbury. As he described his examination of the tiny piece of flesh only one and a half inches in length and less than half an inch wide, one could have heard the proverbial pin drop in the court room. He had the ability, as he always had, to explain the most difficult medical details in terms so simple that they immediately became clear to the jury.

In the case of this alleged scar tissue, he told the Court how he had examined it under the microscope and that at each end of the fragment there were glands, but none in the centre, proving that at some time it had been cut and had not gained its shape through folding. It was a characteristic of Spilsbury that he was so confident about his assertions after his prolonged and detailed investigation to ascertain the truth, that not even a judge could cause him any disquiet.

The Lord Chief Justice, Lord Alverstone, heard the trial of Crippen. Undoubtedly in order to accord the prisoner every possible support in his defence, the Judge queried whether Spilsbury had read about the operation in the newspapers, and also whether he had really given evidence

The Central Criminal Court, Old Bailey, 1841

The " pressing " reserved for non-pleaders. A pleader might lose his estate, but a man pressed to death for not pleading left his estate intact to his heirs

The laſt Dying Speech and Confeſſion, Parentage and Behaviour, of the TWO UNFORTUNATE MALEFACTORS,

Executed this Day before the Debtor's Door, Newgate.

To which is added, The Copy of a moſt excellent Prayer, written and uſed by *Thomas Hunter*, during his Confinement, and is recommended to the Uſe of every Perſon.

Printed and Sold in London.

A broadsheet recording the confessions of Peter Declerk, a Merchant Navy captain convicted of passing a forged bank note, and Thomas Hunter, convicted of burglary

A mass execution at the New Gallows in the Old Bailey

merely to confirm the opinion expressed by his superior, Dr. Pepper.

Very quietly but firmly Dr. Spilsbury told the Judge: " I have an independent position and I am responsible for my own opinion, which has been formed on my own scientific knowledge."

Later the jury went into an adjoining room and each member peered through Spilsbury's microscope so that they could see for themselves where the glands had been cut. This medical evidence finished any chance of the defence succeeding in sowing the seeds of doubt about the identity of the body, despite further witnesses who did their best to disprove the evidence of Dr. Pepper and Dr. Spilsbury.

Then, when during the closing hours of the trial it was shown that a pyjama jacket which had been discovered with the body had been sold to Dr. Crippen and delivered to his house in January 1909, destroying any possible theory of a body buried before he rented the house, the verdict of guilty of murder by administering hyoscin was inevitable.

Quite the most remarkable feature of this remarkable trial was in my view the behaviour of Dr. Crippen. He watched the pathetic remains of his wife being handed around the Court with absolute coolness and without betraying a tremor of emotion. His wisps of sandy hair were neatly brushed across his balding head and I never saw a trace of perspiration, not even during the four hours of his cross-examination, despite the strain shown in his immobile hands. Not once did he hesitate in his answers to the hundreds upon hundreds of searching questions that he was asked. Always he had a plausible answer which fitted in exactly with his own account of what had happened to his wife.

Only when the good name and welfare of his pretty young mistress seemed to be in jeopardy did I notice the slightest sign of worry, but this quickly disappeared. In fact the only emotion he ever showed was a quick sense of humour so that he never failed to smile when some witty remark or amusing comment was made by one of the witnesses.

The jury was absent for only twenty-seven minutes. When they returned with their verdict of guilty, Crippen stood silent and erect, his grey eyes unblinking behind his spectacles. In reply to the usual question as to whether he had anything to say before sentence was passed he asserted once again in a voice of perfect composure that he was innocent.

At the very time that the police were disinterring the remains of Mrs. Crippen in Camden Town, another poisoner was starting to plan a nefarious deed in a house not much more than two miles distant. It was in July 1910 that Frederick Henry Seddon let the top floor of the house he owned at 63 Tollington Park in North London to an eccentric and rather feckless spinster of forty-nine, Eliza Barrow.

Seddon had one ruling passion—the acquisition of money. His main job was the supervision of insurance representatives in North London. The remuneration for a man of his class was good, and the work onerous. But Seddon eagerly grabbed every extra penny from sidelines that he could. He regularly appeared on the stage of local music halls and theatres in crowd scenes, quite content with 2s. 6d. for an evening's work. He rented a tumble-down shop near Finsbury Park and put his wife in it to buy and sell old clothes. He traded in anything and everything, from second-hand sewing machines to slum property, in order to amass more wealth.

His purchase of No. 63 Tollington Park was one of his least successful enterprises. He paid a rather high price for it, and he found that it was difficult to let the rooms at a good figure.

It was only the necessity of getting some return for his money that influenced him to accept Eliza Barrow as a tenant for 12s. a week. It is most unlikely that he could

have known then that the shabby, dirty old woman was, by
Seddon's standards, a person of considerable wealth.

But it did not take him long to find out. Miss Barrow
and Seddon were birds of a feather. They talked, lived and
breathed money. Both boasted about their resources, and
both expressed their views on how to make more money.
Doubtless Seddon listened with great interest, and soon
his plans to gain control of Miss Barrow's assets began to
take shape.

A couple with whom she had been friendly and who had
moved into Seddon's house about the same time as she had
were suddenly given notice. Miss Barrow, who needed a
cheap servant, agreed to let their nephew, a boy of ten,
remain and to sleep in her room.

By the end of the year Miss Barrow's self-appointed
financial adviser had persuaded her to sell almost all her
stock, transfer the property she owned to him and to withdraw the money she had in deposit in a savings bank and
keep it in her cash box. In exchange for an annuity which
Seddon provided for her producing about £3 a week, he
obtained control or possession of almost all her wealth.

The summer of 1911 was the hottest of the century and
there was a considerable amount of epidemic disease
about. When Seddon's doctor was called in to see Miss
Barrow, who had suddenly become unwell, he diagnosed
her trouble as epidemic diarrhoea. The room she lived in
was in a revolting condition and there were myriads of
flies buzzing about, so that the use of arsenical fly-papers
was a perfectly reasonable thing.

The doctor continued to visit his patient daily and for
a fortnight there was no improvement. On September 11
Seddon persuaded Miss Barrow to draw up a will in
which she named the small boy and a niece as her only
beneficiaries and appointed Seddon as sole trustee.

Early in the morning two days later Miss Barrow died.
Her doctor issued a death certificate without inspecting
the body. Seddon promptly made arrangements for the
funeral, explaining to a local undertaker that the woman

had left nothing except £4 in small change. After some argument he persuaded the undertaker to do the job for this amount, less 12s. 6d. commission for Seddon.

Although Seddon swore at his trial that he had written to Miss Barrow's relatives, none of them heard of her death until a week later when a married couple called to see her. Seddon was out at the time and a maid servant said he would be home that evening. When they called again Seddon either would not or could not see them. It was more than a fortnight before the interview took place and if Seddon had only shown a little decency and sympathy nothing further might have been heard of Eliza Barrow. But Seddon was very rude and threatened to drive his visitors from the house.

As regards her money, he said, the £400 which Miss Barrow was supposed to keep in her room simply did not exist. All he had found was a total of £10 and he indicated on a slip of paper that the expense of the funeral and on feeding and clothing the boy had meant that he was £1 1s. 10½d. out of pocket. The relatives went away full of forebodings. They saw the police and the inevitable result was that Miss Barrow's body was exhumed. Arsenic was discovered in the organs and after careful police enquiries Seddon was arrested on December 4, 1911, and his wife in the middle of the following January.

The trial was one of the longest for murder that I have ever witnessed. It lasted ten days. Seldom have I seen a man so completely in control of himself. His utter calmness throughout the trial could only have come from the fact that he was a man without any tender feelings of any kind whatever—a soulless machine existing only for the purpose of amassing wealth.

At the trial he obviously considered himself more acute and brilliant than his own counsel, the prosecution, the Judge and the witnesses.

His detached interest repelled everyone, and Marshall Hall, who defended him, while admitting that he was the ablest man he ever defended on a capital charge, later said that he had no faith in his client, although his legal mind told him that the Crown had a very weak case.

I watched Seddon stand up to a cross-examination which went on for hour after hour. He did not show the slightest fear or betray any emotion by an indecisive answer or a tremor of the voice. Even in reply to his own counsel his words were cold and contemptuous, and his manner of staring at the jury as if they were some sort of insects did not help him.

Only once did I see his absolute serenity momentarily disturbed. Sir Rufus Isaacs (later Lord Reading), the Attorney-General, asked him about some evidence that he had brought Miss Barrow's box of sovereigns from under her bed while she lay there dead and had methodically counted them in the presence of one of his insurance agents.

For once the slow monotone of Seddon's replies changed into a near-shout as he said: " I am not a degenerate. That would make out I am a greedy, inhuman monster or something like a very degenerate man to commit a vile crime such as the prosecution suggest—and bringing the dead woman's money and counting it in the presence of my assistant and flaunting it like that! The suggestion is scandalous! "

He paused for breath, and then with a slight screwing up of his calculating eyes, he added almost as an afterthought: " I would have had all day to count the money."

This brief demonstration of his cunning and greed came late in his long session in the witness box. He was there for three days. Only on one other occasion did his iron nerve show signs of breaking, and that was when police evidence suggested that he had been anxious to know whether his wife was to be arrested, the insinuation being that he might possibly throw doubts as to who had actually administered the poison.

His reaction was immediate and angry. " There is nothing that has hurt me more than this since my arrest," he said. " It has been the greatest trial of my life since she has been arrested and we have neglected our five children."

In fairness to one of the most heartless men who ever stood in the dock at the Old Bailey in my time it must be said that Seddon's regard for his wife and family was consistent and genuine.

At this distance of time it is, of course, normal to think of Seddon as one of the classic poisoners of modern times, but I must stress that during his trial there were considerable doubts as to whether he would be found guilty. In the witness box Mrs. Seddon appeared to me to be a rather frail and stupid woman completely dominated by her husband, but that did not mean that she could not be a willing or coerced partner in crime. Her fear of her husband could account for some of the disquieting explanations that she gave about her actions, but that this was possibly the wrong impression was shown by her activity after she was acquitted. This meek and extremely plain little woman got married within a matter of days after her husband was executed in April 1912, and she made for herself a considerable sum of money by selling to a newspaper a so-called confession, in which she claimed that she had actually seen her husband poison Miss Barrow and had kept silent about it because she was afraid of him.

Within a day of this confession being printed, further statements appeared in rival newspapers in which she denied the story absolutely. As her own words cannot be relied upon the real truth of the Seddon murder will never be known. But her character was more deep than her appearance suggested. I recall the sensation when evidence was given that this woman, going to the undertakers, had insisted on the coffin being opened so that she could kiss the corpse.

But to return to the trial of Seddon. The brilliant medical evidence of Dr. Spilsbury, who proved completely to the jury's satisfaction that Miss Barrow had indeed died from arsenic administered a matter of days before her death, materially helped the jury to reach a decision. They took less than an hour to reach their verdict of guilty against Seddon, while acquitting his wife.

Seddon did not appear to show any interest and I noticed that he had turned his head so an artist on the Press benches who was making a sketch of the scene could see his face to the best advantage.

Mrs. Seddon was, of course, standing beside him in the dock and when the jury acquitted her—as everybody thought they would after the summing up of the Judge, Mr. Justice Bucknill, who indicated that the prosecution had failed to satisfy him of her guilt—he turned to her and before the warders could separate them he had kissed her loudly and affectionately, but he never gave another glance in her direction as she was removed from the dock wailing and weeping hysterically.

He seemed to take no notice of the ritual in preparation for the pronouncement of sentence until the Judge made the customary query as to whether he had anything to say. Patiently the court listened while he gave once again a long and precise account of all his financial negotiations with Miss Barrow.

Even at this terrible moment of his life he was able to itemise every penny and to give precise times and dates when stocks had been transferred and annuities arranged.

Then came the final sensation of all, when he gave the Judge a masonic sign and said before the Great Architect of the Universe he was innocent of murder. This gesture greatly upset the aged Judge who was also a mason. His Lordship's voice faltered and dropped to a whisper. There were tears in his eyes when he reminded the prisoner that though they were both members of the same brotherhood it was a brotherhood which condemned crime.

This reproof of one mason by another did not trouble Seddon at all.

" It does not affect me, Sir. I have a clear conscience ", he said, and when in the final words the Judge begged him to make his peace with God, Seddon retorted: " I am at peace." The square of black cloth was placed on the Judge's head and Seddon was duly sentenced to death.

The prisoner listened to it quite unmoved and carefully did up his overcoat, smoothing the creases. Glancing at the shelf in front of him he picked up the glass of water, took one or two sips from it, and as the warder gently took his arm, he resisted the hold for a second, looking slowly round the court contemptuously and cynically before he turned away.

He appealed against the sentence and it is interesting to know that when this was dismissed a nation-wide petition was started which actually gained more than 100,000 signatures, mostly from men. It was said by the prison authorities that right until the last moment he believed that he would be given a Royal pardon and one of the last statements that he made which was known to the public concerned the reply to his solicitor whom he saw a few hours before he walked to the scaffold.

His question had been as to the amount of money obtained when the furniture and effects of his house were put up to auction. He insisted on knowing the precise figure for almost every item and where some of the bric-a-brac had fetched only a few shillings he said: "That's done it!"

He was more concerned with money than his immortal soul—a sin perhaps which had been with him all his life and had led him to disaster. The feeling remains in my mind that Seddon was condemned by his own mercenary and inhuman attitude in the court as much as by the evidence against him.

In a way, Seddon and his counsel had to prove his innocence rather than the prosecution proving his guilt. Arsenic was certainly present in Eliza Barrow's body, but the medical evidence was not absolutely irrefutable that it was the sole cause of death; still less did the prosecution prove beyond all doubt that the poison came from fly papers, and it was unable to offer any suggestions as to how large doses had been administered to a woman who was by nature suspicious and obstinate, and who was under constant treatment by her doctor at the time. If Seddon had been able to explain away any of these mysteries, and in doing so show he had not been involved there can be no doubt that he would have gone free. Many legal experts thought he would and should do so.

But he did not. His advisers were given no assistance to enable them to fight for him. He would not even apologise for his money-grabbing activities, and it was difficult for any normal man on a jury to accept that a greedy miser of Seddon's type, even though he would have put his hands on every penny no matter how Eliza Barrow had died, might still baulk at murder to assuage his greed for gold.

Someone administered arsenic to the revolting old woman lying in her filth and squalor in that bedroom in Tollington Park. It may have been deliberate, it may have been accidental. Probably Seddon, if he was aware of what was going on would not have felt the slightest tremor of disgust or horror.

If so, he was without doubt an accessory before and after the fact. Whether he was the actual poisoner—or the protector of someone whom in his strange way he loved—will remain an enigma for ever.

CHAPTER FIVE

The Fatal Glitter of Gold

THE DIVIDING LINE BETWEEN A FOOL AND a rogue is often vague. I have often wondered whether Thomas Farrow was one of the most sanctimonious hypocrites who have ever appeared in the Old Bailey dock or whether he was just a ridiculous and small-minded man who had neither the desire nor the ability to protect the fools he defrauded against themselves.

He stood in the dock at a time when crooked financiers were almost queuing up for trial and punishment, yet even with the sense of indignation that the evidence at his trial produced my final reaction was one of pity and contempt —not dislike and disgust.

His trial, in company with his partner and auditor, began on June 6, 1921. Mr. Justice Greer heard the case, and that brilliant advocate Sir Richard Muir led for the prosecution. I suppose that both Judge and jury felt a sort of unwilling sympathy for the little man, as I did, for the sentence of four years' imprisonment was really very light in view of the filching by Farrow and his associate of nearly £3,000,000 of the public's money. I must admit I was perhaps a little biased in the prisoner's favour, for one of my war-time comrades, with whom I had shared many a dugout and talked over a mug of "char" was Farrow's son. I knew that the banker was a kindly and devoted husband and father.

But the money he took came almost entirely from people of very modest means. There must have been at least 50,000 people who lost their pathetically small savings through Farrow. I myself was friendly with some neighbours whom I had invited round for a Christmas Eve drink in 1920. The man, a retired railwayman in his late sixties, had gone to the bank in Cheapside on the previous day to draw out some money for the purchase of a turkey and other festive luxuries—only to find, like thousands of other depositors in seventy-four branches of the Farrow Bank, that the doors were closed and the ominous notice " payments suspended " implied the worst.

In South London there were minor riots, and the police had to drive away the crowds who foolishly if understandably believed that by breaking in they could retrieve what was theirs.

Thomas Farrow was sixty years of age when he appeared at the Old Bailey neatly and quietly dressed in a rather cheap suit, with a moustache which reminded me uncannily of Crippen's, and a lame leg which made him all the more pathetic. That he felt the situation acutely was obvious, but as the story of his life was unfolded at the trial it was only too obvious that he had only himself to blame.

He had been born in Norwich in circumstances which should have ensured an honourable and even distinguished career in law or politics. His parents encouraged him to study for the profession of a solicitor, but he was attracted by the challenge of national legislation and through family influence obtained the post of confidential secretary to W. H. Smith, at that time the respected Leader of the House of Commons. As Farrow was then barely nineteen this was a post that should have almost automatically led to political eminence in due course.

Mr. Smith died about a year after Farrow began to work for him, and the young man easily obtained another secretarial post with the M.P. for Chester, a Mr. Yerburgh, who was active in assisting small farmers with financial aid on reasonable terms of interest. Very rapidly the M.P.'s secretary became better known than his master in this campaign, and at the youthful age of 22 Farrow was a national figure on account of his campaign against the extortionate rates charged by moneylenders to smallholders and similar rural people—a strangely incongruous fame in view of his later activities.

In 1904 he founded the Croydon Mutual Credit Deposit Bank, really a savings club. It developed rapidly and in 1907 Farrow formed Farrow's Bank, with a capital of £1,000,000. The object was to lend money at 10 per cent. to poor but honest persons, while depositors got 5 per cent. interest on their money. Farrow advertised his bank principally in religious journals, and his scheme received the official blessing of Bishops of the Church of England and leaders of the Non-conformist Church. To encourage savings until the minimum balance of £10 could be handed over he issued thousands of little steel safes free of charge. His customers he called Farrovians, and they received a chatty little magazine telling them how well everything was going, with uplifting articles on the virtues of simple living and saving for a rainy day.

It must be said that Farrow himself largely practised what he preached. He had a modest house in Sussex and kept precise hours at the headquarters of his bank just like his most junior employee, and there was never a hint of the blatant extravagance which marked the lives of his contemporaries in the field of fraud.

Except perhaps for the first year of the bank's life the balance sheet appears always to have been faked. In the final one things were in such chaos that the published profit of £22,000 was in fact a loss of £2,200,000. How long Farrow would have managed to continue is a matter of conjecture. He was nearing the end of his tether when an American financier started negotiations to acquire a controlling interest in what was evidently a flourishing British financial institution. Farrow was so incurably optimistic that he apparently believed that he could pull wool over the eyes of an expert with the glibness that had convinced thousands of ordinary folk.

He was, of course, wrong. The American's accountants reported that something was amiss. The Board of Trade was consulted, and the result was the closing of the bank's doors and the arrest of Farrow and his partner Crotch.

According to Farrow's evidence in Court, the whole

thing was a regrettable mistake—a mistake that had steadily increased the annual losses from £11,000 in the second year of the bank's existence to a record loss of £203,000 in the final period before Nemesis overtook them. Perhaps I was wrong in feeling sorry for the little man with his martyred pleas that he hadn't taken a penny of profit for himself beyond his salary of £1,500 a year and that he had worked so hard that he had never once managed to have a holiday.

A glimpse of the real man beneath the humbugging facade came when he was jolted from his meek politeness in the witness box as prosecuting counsel lashed him for dishonesty.

" I'm not an accountant ", he retorted in a burst of temper. " I'm an idealist, an organiser and an optimist."

It was almost impossible to believe that he had for thirteen years stifled his conscience with these feelings of virtue. That he could protest in this way at a time when tens of thousands of people faced ruin through his frauds indicated what a hypocrite he really was.

The atmosphere of solemnity in the Old Bailey can usually curb the ebullience of the most vivacious and irresponsible of witnesses. Its effect on defendants is to destroy within minutes most of their clever little plans for lying their way to freedom.

But there are a few people—very few—who seem to flourish in the legal aura as if it was the perfect setting for their personalities. The few great lawyers who have left their mark in judicial history in this half century are among them. Judges, by their very impersonality, are not affected except perhaps Mr. Justice Avory and Lord Goddard, both of whom shine in my memory through their brilliance of occasional interjected comment and question and in their summing up.

But I know of only one defendant who seemed to glory in his period of notoriety in the Court—and this was all the more remarkable because he must have known beyond any doubt that he was as guilty as a man could be and would inevitably walk out of the Court to serve a long term of imprisonment.

That man was Horatio Bottomley. He was, at the time I politely smiled at one of his sallies told in a voice that boomed and echoed in the corridor outside the court room, one of the most hated men in the country—a transition from his more accustomed role as a national hero and benefactor.

It was within an hour of complete disaster for this ageing rogue that he made the sauciest challenge that the old walls of the Central Criminal Court can have ever heard.

He was, following his invariable custom, conducting his own case, and had been haranguing the jury in a fashion I thought unique until talking pictures arrived years afterwards with their attorneys doing just the same thing in American court room dramas.

Horatio Bottomley, his puffy face mottled red with effort, his calculating little eyes flashing with indignation, pointed a chubby finger at the Sword of Justice hanging on the wall above the Judge, Mr. Justice Salter, and then he told the jury: "You'll never convict me. The man is not yet born who would convict me on these charges. It is unthinkable. That Sword of Justice would fall from its scabbard if you returned a verdict of guilty against me."

Although the evidence of Bottomley's fantastic and heartless frauds belied this brash claim to innocence it was noted that as the foreman stood to give the jury's verdict of guilty after a mere half hour's deliberation, several people in the Court, including the jury, involuntarily glanced at the sword.

Bottomley didn't spare a moment on it, of course. He had probably forgotten the bluff as he seemed to have forgotten his crooked activities. For once he was silent as the Judge sentenced him to seven years' penal servitude.

He attempted to produce a look of indignation and pathos as he was led to the cells—but there could be little sympathy for the man. Most of his thousands of victims must have considered that seven years' deprivation of freedom was not a great price to pay for a series of crimes spread over more than thirty years and more than 250 appearances in the Courts, at most of which he had been the victor.

Horatio Bottomley's vices were unbridled ambition and unreasonable vanity. Today psychologists would say that his birth and childhood were the causes. He was born in the East End of London in 1860 of very poor parents. But they were decent, law-abiding folk even though in the later years Bottomley used to boast that he was the illegitimate son of a famous Victorian free-thinker and politician. His parents were unable to look after him and he grew up in a Birmingham orphanage.

At fifteen he was back in London, working as an office boy in a solicitor's office—his introduction to the legal world with its traps and its loopholes. Court hearings fascinated him and he avidly studied shorthand in order to get a job as a court reporter. He did comparatively well and at the age of twenty got married.

His first known fraud occurred in 1889, when he formed a bogus company alleged to own publishing rights and printing plant in Vienna. He managed to get hold of nearly £100,000 from this company, tucked the sum out of reach, and went bankrupt.

Five years later he was a flourishing company promoter, offering his dupes gold mines in remote areas of Australia. As his " experts " sadly reported that one mine had proved barren a new company took over its assets and started digging somewhere else. In four years there were nearly twenty of these companies, with nominal capital running into millions. Of course, only a fraction of the shares were ever sold, but even so Bottomley must have netted a fortune out of them before the criticism in the Press warned him that it would be advisable to seek new fields of enterprise.

But first he felt entitled to a little rest and recreation. The accession of Edward VII had turned London into the gayest city on earth. Bottomley, now in his early forties, was one of the best-known figures on the outer fringes of London society. He was at every race meeting. His champagne parties were a feature of every theatrical first night. His bets and extravagances were a byword.

It was then that he aimed higher than ever before. He got himself adopted as prospective M.P. for South Hackney, and in 1906 was elected. In the same year he founded *John Bull* (since that time, of course, brought under the control and ownership of entirely different and reputable publishers) and used it for two purposes: the promotion of competitions and for indirect blackmail. The paper attacked small crooks and exposed activities which Bottomley knew only too well were crooked. But bigger fish escaped the *John Bull* net by an arrangement involving hush money.

He was in and out of Court at this time, defending libel actions, usually successfully, and winning legal arguments against some of his dupes who thought to get their money back.

In the year that he became the respected Independent Liberal Member of Parliament for South Hackney he appeared on sixteen occasions in Carey Street as one or another of his companies went bankrupt, while at the same time he was busy forming new and equally phoney enterprises in which the shares were sold several times over. All was grist to his mill. He would take the £100 life savings off one of his constituents as eagerly as sums ranging from £10,000 to £90,000 from wealthier but equally unwise investors.

He seemed to have a charmed life so far as prosecution for fraud was concerned. Even when in 1911 a succession of suits forced him to go bankrupt once more, with liabilities of £213,000 and assets of £50,000, nothing more serious occurred than an insistent request from his party leaders that he should resign his seat in the Commons.

He concentrated on running *John Bull* and in particular promoting its competitions. I have always had many friends in Fleet Street, travelling to and from my home with journalists and meeting them at lunch time. I remember the stories they told in those days of how Bottomley would take a chorus girl to lunch at the Savoy and inform her that she was to be the first prize winner in next week's competition, of the ex-convicts, jockeys, and racing touts who attained sudden affluence as they shared the prize loot with the promoter of the contest. As the prizes sometimes reached £25,000, which was always amply covered by the entry fees, this was a not unprofitable source of income.

Probably the outbreak of war saved him from prosecution as the complaints and gossip increased. Yet he had the effrontery, just when reverses had destroyed the optimism of the first few weeks that " the war should be over by Christmas ", to announce a competition, with a first prize of £10,000 and £40,000 in smaller prizes, for the competitor who most accurately forecast the size of the indemnity against Germany in the Peace Treaty. The entry fee was a shilling, but no competitor ever heard the result of this contest, the closing date of which was, had they but known it, nearly four years off.

His activities as a speaker at recruiting meetings, for which he demanded exorbitant fees, brought him more fame than ever before. I was by then a soldier in the Middle East, and never heard him speak. Undoubtedly his rabble-rousing brand of hysterical patriotism sent tens of thousands of men rushing to the nearest recruiting office, and I can recall some of the bitter things my comrades in the desert had to say about this well-fed civilian who trumpeted about the glory of war and the privilege of becoming a hero in it.

The advent of conscription in 1917 meant the virtual end of his source of income as a recruiting lecturer, whereupon he changed his patriotic efforts to the enrolment of money for the war effort instead of men. In January 1918 he launched through the medium of *John Bull* a War Stock Combination which was a scheme to buy savings certificates and to pay prizes in a draw, the money being borrowed against the interest accruing in five years' time from the savings certificates. Bottomley took care that the scheme

3

had the appearance of being semi-official, and he netted £80,000 from this particular campaign.

He paid a few prizes and was looked upon as such a patriotic benefactor of his country that in the 1918 election he easily got himself re-elected to Parliament, again for South Hackney.

The success of the first savings scheme—he still had no need to worry about handing over certificates to subscribers as these were allegedly held by some mysterious trustees—tempted him to launch another in 1919: the gigantic Victory Bond Club. No one ever discovered how much the gullible public invested in this scheme, but Bottomley himself never denied the figure of £500,000.

At intervals he launched further schemes of the same kind, and although the end of the spendthrift period of 1919 with the short post-war trade boom and the demobilisation of a million or so men and women with gratuities to spend meant that the succeeding schemes did not net so much, he must have extracted at least a further £200,000 from the public.

The end was near. Bottomley, living like an Indian prince, with a magnificent Surrey home where the horses' stables were fashioned from rare woods imported from every continent, starting factories, becoming the most spectacular gambler on the turf that the bookmakers had known for a decade, was in fact vainly struggling to extricate himself from a tightening net.

Some of his victims were fighting back. There were some pamphlets being published exposing him for the crook he was that got him on the horns of a dilemma. Either he had to sue the writers for libel and risk some unpleasant truths emerging in Court, or else he had to remain silent and thus confirm everything that was alleged.

And so, in May 1922, he found himself in the Old Bailey. He arrived on the first day of the hearing after a champagne breakfast and wearing his sixty-guinea morning suit. He left on the last day for a convict's garb and the evening mug of cocoa.

His last financial deal was with the State: he applied, a broken and ailing old man of seventy-three, for an old age pension. He died shortly afterwards, in 1933.

1922 was the great year for fraud trials at the Old Bailey. The case which came on in November of that year had been expected for some time, and the extent of the defendant's alleged defalcations was known before the sensational Bottomley trial.

The man concerned in this instance was Gerald Lee Bevan, an aristocrat by appearance and birth. Among the staff of the Central Criminal Court whose duty it was to look after him during the hearing of his case he was known as " His Excellency ". He somehow managed to regard the warder who brought his lunch as a head waiter, and indeed the meal was eaten with all the delicacy and mannerisms of a guest in a fashionable hotel. As if by right, he waited for doors to be opened as if the court attendants were footmen, and his dress was impeccable.

All this exalted behaviour did not disguise the fact that Gerald Lee Bevan was by then a rather ridiculous figure, adding to his record of financial sinning a tawdry tale of flight and hiding which had kept all Europe agog for months.

He was the son of the chairman of one of the country's biggest banks. He had been educated at Eton and Oxford, and in 1894, when he was only twenty-four, his father obtained him a partnership in one of the greatest stockbroking firms in the City of London, the old-established concern of Ellis and Co., which handled the investments of many of the most illustrious and richest families in the country. The firm's turnover was colossal—in excess of £12,000,000 a year by 1912, when Bevan became the senior of the five partners and the principal shareholder.

His position made him a wealthy man, and there was really no need for dishonesty to tempt him to increase his income. True he lived expensively, but not in the flamboyant and extravagant manner of, say, Bottomley.

He was married to a cousin of Austen Chamberlain and

had both a West End and a country house. He collected
first editions, pictures and porcelain—but was regarded
by the trade in these objects as a shrewd and moderate
buyer. He was certainly not what antique dealers call
"a repository", on whom practically any desirable piece
could be foisted at an inflated price.

Perhaps his trouble was women. His children had grown
up, and he was in his late forties—a physically attractive
and virile man. There was a French mistress on whom
reputedly he spent a small fortune; other women wheedled
sufficient out of him to set them up for life.

Whatever the motive for his deliberate development of
his firm's activities beyond the accustomed dealing in
reputable shares, he was ambitiously starting new enterprises as early as 1908, and then he arranged for his firm
to acquire big holdings in the City Equitable Insurance
Company in 1916. Until then this eight-year-old concern
had progressed modestly and cautiously under the policy
of its board which included a number of distinguished
persons.

Bevan developed the company's activities so vigorously
that the premium income of the pre-war year of 1913 of
£83,000 rose by 1920-21 to £3,400,000. Through his firm
or friends, he himself held shares worth £800,000. They
were paying dividends of up to 250 per cent. Bevan soon
had to disguise the true state of affairs—that the impressive
assets of the insurance company depended on loans from
Ellis and Co., at the time of the crash amounting to somewhere around half a million pounds, which, as the stock
market was weakening, was merely a paper valuation.

He had to get real money from somewhere, because most
of the resources in both the insurance company and the
stockbroking firm were evaporating. He floated a public
company to take over City Equitable's companies. Within
six months the firm was dying, and a directors' meeting was
held at which a thorough investigation of the books was
ordered. The facts, which everyone seemed to have ignored
till then, were only too obvious. City Equitable filed a

petition in bankruptcy, and a few days later Ellis and Co. were "hammered" on the Stock Exchange. The deficiencies in the books of Bevan's companies were estimated at about £3,000,000.

Bevan was not there to read the sensational headlines in the evening papers. On the night of February 8 he had rushed to Croydon airport and paid a large fee to a pilot to fly him out of the country. It was damning evidence of his own sense of guilt, for a night flight in mid-winter across the Channel in 1922 was an expedition that few would have tackled. That he had prepared for such an eventuality as this was proved by the fact that the emigration people had authorised him to leave the country as he had a valid passport which gave his name as Leon Vernier, of French origin.

The flight occurred just twelve hours before a warrant for his arrest was issued. Police forces throughout Europe were alerted and a newspaper offered a big reward for information on his hiding place. He managed to evade arrest for four months, when the Viennese police questioned a man with obviously dyed hair and a newly-grown beard who was sitting enjoying the sunshine with a pretty girl at a pavement café. He rushed off as the police approached, but was caught after a brief chase. After serving a sentence in an Austrian prison for illegal entry into Austria he was brought back by Scotland Yard detectives in the autumn.

The Old Bailey trial was before Mr. Justice Avory. The inevitable verdict of guilty brought a sentence of seven years' penal servitude. After his release he emigrated to Cuba, where he started a wine and spirits business, prospering modestly until his death in 1936.

One autumn evening in 1928 I took a favourite walk of mine—along the Victoria Embankment from Blackfriars to Charing Cross and on to Westminster. It was just after the homegoing rush hour, and the gas lamps had just come on, their light reflected in the dirty water of the river and on the glistening pavements, for it had been raining until half an hour before I left my office at the Old Bailey.

Not many people were walking at the time, but I saw ahead of me a man of middle height, slim in his light-weight coat, enjoying the scene as much as I was. I was interested in him, for I had seen a limousine pull across the tramlines that existed then on the riverside of the Embankment, when this distinguished man got out. I had expected that he was about to visit the RNVR training ship or possibly would cross the road and enter the Inns of Court. He was obviously " something in the City ", and something important at that. Business men of that kind are not usually tempted by a stroll along the Embankment.

He walked on quite quickly until we came to the bridge at Charing Cross. There the usual group of nondescripts were hanging around, awaiting the time when it would be safe to doss down in the Villiers Street tunnel or obtain some refreshment from the charity coffee stall that arrived during the evening.

I saw the man put his hand in his pocket and hand some coins to a woman sitting on a bench. I saw him cross to the river wall and do the same to an old man who was staring out across the river. He continued to distribute alms as far as the landing stage at Westminster. It was there that I saw a policeman I knew because he had been a witness in a robbery case at the Old Bailey a week or so before. He saw me looking at the well-dressed Good Samaritan and grinned.

" Seen him handing out half-crowns, have you? " he said. " He is often down here, a real good sort. He has some way of knowing the genuine cases and I've never known him hand out help to the phoneys I know because we have facts about them on record. It isn't always just a bob or two. There have been miners and hunger marchers who have got their railway ticket back home, and something for a batch of groceries for their families into the bargain.

" Who is he? We have tried to find out, in a friendly

way, of course, but he has always smiled and said that he prefers to remain anonymous. He's a decent bloke, all right."

The next time I saw that "decent bloke" was in the dock at the Old Bailey. His name was Clarence Hatry, who was told by the Judge, Mr. Justice Avory, that he stood "convicted on your own confession of the most appalling frauds which have ever besmirched the commercial reputation of this country, frauds more serious than any of the great frauds on the public of the past fifty years."

I cannot pretend to understand the path which this gentle and brilliant-minded man of early middle age took through the jungle of high finance. Indeed I doubt whether any individual following the fantastic evidence of the long trial could fully appreciate motive and method. Certainly the unravelling of the tangled web and the salvaging of something would have been virtually impossible without the willing aid of the man who was put on trial.

Clarence Hatry had started his career as an insurance broker, and it was during the burst of company re-organisations and new projects after the First World War that he entered the exclusive circle of high finance. Some of the companies he controlled at this time are today sound and important entities ; but others crashed in ruins. He was perhaps too ambitious and too imaginative. He visualised vast amalgamations of competing firms as the best method of survival in a world where Britain's industrial competitors would yearly grow more powerful. He knew no better than the financiers of any other country that the world was tottering to a terrible depression beyond the control of governments, let alone private individuals. He lost a a mountain of investors' money, but probably he was the biggest individual loser: almost the whole of his fortune amassed over a dozen years—nearly £750,000—went with the rest.

He had been unlucky rather than unwise ; certainly there was no question that till then he had been dishonest.

Even so, lesser men would have retired from the exacting arena of finance. But Clarence Hatry, who truthfully said that his great pleasure in life was work, started all over again. In 1925 the Austin Friars Trust was formed, its object to finance another trust to gain control of scores of department stores up and down the country.

From the magnificent Pinner's Hall in Austin Friars Hatry expanded his trusts to cater for municipal loans, to launch new industries, to finance automatic machine enterprises, and—most ambitious of all—to rationalise the iron and steel industry. For the last idea he had to find the gigantic sum of £8,000,000.

He was able to obtain all but £900,000 of this sum, by mortgaging all possible assets and by obtaining every loan he could. If he had accepted defeat in June 1929, creditors would have doubtless forced the whole Hatry set-up into liquidation and the iron and steel scheme would have fallen through. No one would have hinted that the financier had been guilty of any illegal action, and it would have been just a case of the history of the 1914-1920 period repeating itself.

But neither Hatry nor his fellow-directors would admit defeat. At a momentous Sunday conference in the lounge of Hatry's house near Park Lane, with its swimming pool and luxurious gymnasium, the desire to raise money by hook or by crook tempted them to borrow on scrip certificates worth just the value of the paper they were printed on. Loans floated by the Hatry group on behalf of three towns, Gloucester, Swindon and Wakefield, provided the means of subterfuge, and nearly £800,000 were thereby illegally borrowed on worthless securities. In addition, a sum in excess of £800,000 was withheld temporarily from the municipalities on the excuse that the stock market was passing through a brief depression and it would be mutually beneficial to wait awhile.

Thus Hatry had the cash reserves to complete the purchase of the iron and steel shares, and it might well have been that with the formation of the new organisation the sale of shares in it would have produced more than sufficient cash to repay the borrowers on the fictitious scrip as well as to meet the delayed payments to the municipalities. But rumour grew that something was wrong. Panic broke out on the Stock Exchange and there was an avalanche of selling of securities in all the Hatry companies.

The banks were asked to help. They naturally desired to investigate the books, whereupon Clarence Hatry and his colleagues, with the exception of one foreign-born director who fled the country, gave themselves up to the police. The total deficiencies amounted to £13,500,000.

Hatry was sentenced to fourteen years' imprisonment, but was released by the Home Secretary in a little over nine years.

All the famous cases of fraud during the past half century at the Old Bailey have had a direct result in improving the powers of the law to protect investors. It would now be utterly impossible for anyone to thrive on fraud for half a lifetime, as Farrow did, and no one could found the fantastic and fraudulent companies which Bottomley foisted on a gullible public.

Just as we are unlikely to see financial kings who rise with meteor-like rapidity to the millionaire class, so the big-time financial rogue is a memory of the bad old days.

Such frauds as do occur are today intricate manipulations usually designed to find or create loopholes in taxation and similar official curbs on unrestricted money-making. Compared with the millions involved in the classical cases I have described, today's ill-gotten gains are almost trivial, despite the infinitely more intricate methods adopted to obtain them.

Typical of the post-war financial exploit that runs foul of the law was the export china case which lasted for no less than forty-one days at the Old Bailey—the longest hearing known to the Court up to that time. It came after a month's proceedings at Bow Street.

The Judge who heard this remarkable case and made legal history by his wonderfully lucid summing up of the enormous amount of evidence was Mr. Justice Glynn Jones.

The story began in 1947 when a group of business people worked out a scheme for placing decorated china on the home market by a system of diversions of supplies made for export. It is a symptom of the rigorous control which is now part of the life of the country that this could be a serious offence.

For three years the system worked well, but in 1950 the Board of Trade realised that figures of production for export and those for actual exports showed big discrepancies. A preliminary check indicated that goods to the value of about £65,000 had got on to the home market, and this was probably a fraction of the total value.

The details of the conspiracy were not easy to unravel. Scotland Yard's best men took three years to obtain sufficient evidence to justify prosecution and they travelled many thousands of miles through the length and breadth of Britain to examine nine thousand documents and produce a report which was as long as this book.

The methods the detectives revealed were ingenious: a master-mind controlling a dozen people who set up trading companies arranged for export licences to be obtained for decorated china and earthenware. These licences, covered by guarantees that the goods were going overseas, enabled manufacturers to supply the required goods. The makers were, of course, quite innocent parties.

They made the china, crated it, and duly despatched on instructions to various docks. There, instead of going aboard ship, the goods were collected and in due course provided with faked export reject numbers. Within a week or two they were on sale to the public.

The Old Bailey dock has seen many remarkable people in it, but rarely I think a dozen prisoners who seemed so like perfectly respectable citizens. If ever there were men who represented the public school type these were them. Indeed, they had all been to a public school, although this had not prevented five having previous convictions. Three

Queen's Counsel and seventeen juniors for the defence packed the Court, and there were, of course, expert and police witnesses galore.

The hearing was frankly boring in its interminable detail of fictitious invoices, bewildering delivery notes, addresses of consignees which did not exist, and explanations of the way the movement of the goods became submerged in a welter of barter from one firm to another. But the illicit profits which had accrued were obvious. Probably the order to the defendants who were found guilty—all but two of them—to pay costs amounting to £15,000 hurt as much as the prison sentences which ranged from five years to nine months.

CHAPTER SIX

Trials for Espionage and Treachery

DURING THE FIRST WORLD WAR TWELVE
spies were found guilty and were shot in the grounds of
the Tower of London, and another committed suicide. I
was on active service for the major part of the war and
knew nothing of these dramas of justice—with one exception. Colonel Carl Lody, the first spy of 1914-18, was
tried while I was awaiting orders to report to the Army.
Three judges tried this remarkable man behind locked
doors. It was a new experience for the Old Bailey staff,
but one to become all too familiar afterwards.

During the Second World War I was on duty in the
Old Bailey during all the sensational but secret spy trials.

I find that many people have the strangest ideas of the
procedure in these cases. First and foremost it should be
stressed that no matter how horrifying the treachery
involved the procedure of arrest and trial is the same as for
any other crime. Until the Judge pronounces sentence
the defendant is deemed innocent; and he has full facilities
to prepare his defence. Perhaps the only difference from
the privileges of any other prisoner is that a spy is not
allowed to write or receive letters nor to receive visitors
other than his legal advisers.

When a suspected spy was arrested during the war he
was normally taken to Bow Street Police Station, where
special cells were maintained. This rule normally applied
no matter where in the United Kingdom the arrest took
place.

The searching of the prisoner was naturally more
rigorous. He would be completely stripped and his body,
teeth, and hair searched. Not for a moment of the day or
night would he be left alone. Daily medical examinations
were made, and everything which could be used to commit

76

suicide was withdrawn. In the last war no spy managed to evade justice by destroying himself after arrest.

When an espionage trial at the Old Bailey took place we inevitably found the atmosphere of the Court and the routine of our duties materially changed. There were cells in the basement specially checked before prisoners were put inside them, and three warders sat with every man charged with espionage.

Everybody who entered the building had to be provided with special passes—Judge, jury, counsel, witnesses and ordinary officials. The trial was usually arranged for the final days of the session to minimise any possible contact with other prisoners. Police officers attached to the Special Branch screened him as he moved from the cells to the dock and guarded him while he was in Court. On some occasions there were as many as ten guards to ensure that some Nazi fanatic did not make a foolhardy but dangerous gesture of defiance before he was found guilty.

The first modern spy trial, which was an ominous shadow of the black treachery to come, occurred on March 5, 1936, before Mr. Justice Graves-Lord. The prisoner was a gentle-looking and serious man of forty-two. Probably only the British Secret Service knew how dangerous this deceptively meek and polite German really was.

He was charged with making a sketch plan of the R.A.F. station at Manston in Kent calculated to be useful to a foreign country ; and conspiring with Marian Emig, a German subject, to commit offences against the Official Secrets Act.

His name was Dr. Hermann Goertz, and he stated that his occupation was that of a lawyer. He also claimed that he wrote novels. At the time of his arrest he was living at Broadstairs, close to the Manston fighter station, and he protested that he had come to Britain just for a holiday.

The holiday was a long one, and his choice of beauty spots strange. At first he had lived at Mildenhall, the site of the R.A.F.'s biggest station for testing new aircraft at that time. After his removal to Broadstairs he enjoyed visiting the coastal areas of Kent on his motor cycle, stopping to take his photographs and make his sketches at Lympne, Hawkinge, and the North Foreland. All these places were either aerodromes or the sites for the radar stations just being constructed.

The Secret Service had been watching Goertz for some time. While he made a brief visit to Germany his bungalow was visited and as a result he was arrested when he returned to Britain.

At his trial Goertz admitted freely that he had flown fighters in the First World War for Germany and had afterwards worked as an intelligence officer in the Luftwaffe. His defence was that as an ex-airman he was interested in aerodromes and aeroplanes and did not know that it was illegal to tour round them. As regards the sketches and photographs, these, he said, were background material for an adventure novel he intended to write.

Goertz was found guilty and sentenced to four years' imprisonment. By good conduct he was free by the autumn of 1938, and after war broke out he became one of the German agents dropped by parachute in Eire. He was interned in 1944 until September 1946. A few months later, when his appeal against an extradition order which would have meant his return to the Allied zone in Western Germany was dismissed, he bit on a phial of cyanide and killed himself.

Another remarkable story of German activities within Britain was told that during the trial of three people—including a woman—in June 1940, on a charge of intelligence with the enemy.

The woman was Marie Louise Ingram, who had been living in Southsea at the time of her arrest. She had been a British subject by marriage for eighteen years, and although working as a maidservant in the residence of a British naval officer when the security net was tightened around her, she was in fact a woman of good German family. Her father was a highly placed executive on the

German State Railways and her brother-in-law a member of the Nazi High Command.

Mrs. Ingram, an extremely plump woman of forty-two when she was tried at the Old Bailey, was unwise enough to spread her views on Nazi supremacy to a house painter working on her employer's home. The workman felt very suspicious about a woman with a foreign accent condemning the Jews and Mr. Churchill, and praising the British Union of Fascists. He kept quiet so as to hear more. He was given the address of a local official of a Fascist organisation, which he duly joined—but not until he had reported Mrs. Ingram's conversation to the local police. It was soon obvious that the group was endeavouring to collect military information, that it planned to assist enemy parachutists, and dreamed of getting conspirators into the local defence organisations.

One defendant was discharged through lack of evidence, the second was sent to prison for fourteen years, and Mrs. Ingram received a sentence of ten years. She was shouting " Heil Hitler " as she was led from the Court to the cells.

The first convictions on the capital charge of espionage in time of war began on November 2, 1940—at the height of the blitz on London. There were two prisoners, Josef Waldberg, a twenty-five-year-old German from Mainz, and Karl Meier, a native of Coblenz, aged twenty-four, and a Dutchman, Charles van den Kieboom.

The trial was held in camera and no details of the nature of the prisoners' activities in espionage were issued by the Home Office. It has since become known that they were landed secretly in Britain in the autumn of 1940 and roamed about the marshlands on the Kent coast, sometimes going further afield and sleeping in bombed buildings. Their job was to listen to careless talk, and to check on factories and military units. Well provided with English money and bringing a portable transmitter, which could be packed away in two haversacks, they gave themselves away because radio fixes could be taken on their powerful set when they broadcast information back to occupied France every night.

They were typically well trained spies. All spoke fluent English, and all implicity believed that their dangerous duties would be of short duration because the Nazi invasion would ensure their rescue and a good reward for their work. The time of their rescue, incidentally, had been stated by their masters to be October 1940—a promise they no doubt pondered on when they were arrested by British officers in a free Britain more than a month after the dateline. Kieboom appealed against the death sentence, but like his two fellow conspirators he suffered the extreme penalty.

Probably the most thrilling spy drama of the war began on a spring night in 1941 when a Dornier seaplane, flying just above the waves so as to evade the searching eyes of the radar stations, came down on the water a few miles off Kinnaird Head on the Banffshire coast. Two agents got into a rubber dinghy and rowed ashore. Well equipped with English money, speaking faultless English, and trained to the last detail about the geography of Scotland, they managed to get well away from their landing place before dawn broke, separating so that the likelihood of complete failure of their mission was minimised.

Foolishly, one of them went to a small station where every local passenger was known to the railway staff. A porter chatted to the stranger but refrained from showing too much curiosity. Before the train arrived the official had telephoned to a superior at a main station and the result was that before the train reached Aberdeen detectives had boarded it and questioned the traveller. His identity card was so perfectly forged that nothing seemed amiss, but unfortunately for him a small case he was carrying was a portable radio transmitter. The man was eventually identified as Werner Waelti.

His movements were traced back to the point of his arrival and in the sea was found the partly damaged rubber dinghy. The destruction system had failed to work properly. It was obvious that the dinghy was made to hold more than one man and the search for a possible companion of Waelti began. The existence of a second man moving about Scotland on that spring morning was soon proved. Many people had wondered about him even if they had not suspected that he was a spy. Eventually the trail led to Edinburgh, where a man carrying a Danish passport and a seaman's certificate was arrested after a struggle.

The authorities were able to show that his papers were forged, and they believed the man was in fact Karl Druecke, a thirty-six-year-old SS officer and one of the specially trained assassins of the Gestapo.

He was tried at the Old Bailey in June 1941, before Mr. Justice Asquith, where he persisted in claiming that his entry into Britain was for personal reasons unconnected with espionage. But spies, like thieves, are prone to fall out, and his fellow agent Waelti told the whole tale. Both were found guilty and executed.

An intelligent member of the public, suspecting a seemingly innocent person during an ordinary chat, prevented Waelti and Druecke from succeeding. A similar action destroyed in a few hours the carefully laid plans of the enemy to get into the very heart of the British war organism —Whitehall. This agent was landed by parachute during comparatively mild air raid activity during the night of May 13-14, 1942.

The plane came low, dropping the agent, Karl Richter, in the wooded and pasture country beside the Great North Road near Hatfield. Richter found a dense coppice and with a trowel buried his parachute in the soft loam. Nearby he covered up his equipment, which included a radio set, iron rations, money and maps of the London area.

Shortly before dusk he made for the road with the intention of walking to London. A lorry driver pulled up to ask him the way to a village. Richter naturally did not know and he became so confused that he forgot to disguise his German accent. The lorry driver drove on and when he saw a policeman he told him about the mysterious stranger walking along the road a mile or so back. The policeman was a war reserve constable and he soon found and arrested him.

The trial lasted four days, indicating that Richter was no ordinary spy. It was generally believed that he had come for a special assignment of murdering war leaders of an Allied government in London. But no details of the case were forthcoming beyond the grim announcement in the following December that Richter had been hanged at Wandsworth Prison.

Spies like these, whatever one's feelings about the treacherous nature of their work, were brave men. They came secretly into enemy country and did their best to carry out orders. If there is a code of behaviour in the ruthless secret war that is carried on behind the front lines in times of hostilities they did at least observe it.

There can be nothing but a feeling of contempt when the hand of friendship is grasped with the deliberate intention of exploiting tolerance and succour to the ultimate destruction of the provider.

Yet this was the policy of two spies tried at the Old Bailey in 1942. The hearings were, of course, in camera and no details could be published until the war ended. The first trial was of Alphonse Timmermann, executed under the Treachery Act, which since the trial of Mrs. Ingram enabled the death sentence to be pronounced instead of the imprisonment under the old Defence of the Realm Acts.

Timmermann and three other men were picked up by a British Navy patrol vessel in the North Sea. They were in a fishing smack and said that they were members of the Belgian Underground who had escaped because the Gestapo had become aware of their identity.

The men were carefully screened by both British and Belgian counter-espionage agents. All were provisionally cleared. Three joined the Belgian forces in Britain and Timmermann got a post with the Belgian Government in

London. For a time all went well, but a chance meeting with an agent who had recently returned from work in Brussels caused the first suspicion that all was not as it appeared. The agent said that he believed Timmermann to have been an employee of the Gestapo in Belgium.

In his rooms damning evidence of his duplicity was discovered, and he was arrested. The escape of the fishing smack had been permitted by the Germans, even though three of the men in the boat were genuine patriots.

Timmermann probably got very little information of value out of the country before he was caught. Another agent using the patriot refugee idea had no better luck. Johannes Dronkers, a Dutch seaman in his forties and an expert telegraphist, was picked up in a small sailing boat off the English coast just after dawn on a May morning in 1942. The little vessel was proudly flying the flag of the Netherlands. His joy at being rescued was so great that he burst into the song "Tipperary" in excellent English. He had a scrap of paper signed by known leaders of the Dutch Resistance, which pronounced Dronkers a member of the Underground and in imminent danger of arrest by the Gestapo. The most careful scrutiny of this document and prolonged cross-examination of the man revealed no flaw in the story. In due course Dronkers was told that he was a free man. He then began to organise the scheme for which he had been sent to Britain with the carefully forged papers and perfect story of his career—which was to use the BBC overseas programmes to transmit coded messages.

Dronkers cultivated the friendship of the officials in charge of the programme *Radio Oranje,* which was sponsored by the Netherlands Government in London. He found, to his surprise and excitement, that his suggestion about broadcasting a message of greeting to his old comrades was accepted and a time arranged. He wrote his brief script and in the usual way submitted it for timing and censorship. Still everything appeared to be all right. The broadcast was scheduled and Dronkers duly arrived at the underground studio to give his talk. He spoke into the microphone—which unknown to him was dead. He was detained immediately afterwards, charged with espionage.

His trial was held in camera at the Old Bailey on November 13, 1942, before Mr. Justice Wrottesley. He appealed against the verdict of guilty, the grounds being that he had been forced by the Gestapo to work as a spy. The appeal was dismissed and he paid the extreme penalty a month later.

The almost total failure of these "refugee spies" to escape the British security net did not weaken the enemy's determination to exploit this method of getting agents into Britain. In the summer of 1943 one of them actually arrived in an RAF transport aircraft. He was a young ex-officer of the Belgian Army who had crossed occupied France, got into neutral Spain and had appealed to the British Embassy in Madrid to help him to get to Britain to resume the fight against his country's oppressors.

The man, who gave his name as Pierre Neukermanns, was emaciated as were all those who had escaped from some German prison camp. His story of imprisonment after the surrender of the Belgian Army and his subsequent forced labour on Nazi defences in Belgium was plausible and familiar. His account of his work with the Belgian Underground tallied with all the details kept to check such stories. He was cleared by the Embassy and flown to Britain.

He passed the first screening in London with flying colours and he was allowed to take a staff job with the Free Belgian Army. Meantime the difficult task of checking his story with patriots in Belgium slowly produced the real facts. He had indeed been a Belgian Army officer in 1939, but after his country's defeat he had obtained special privileges by declaring himself a Nazi sympathiser. Back in Belgium, he had joined the Underground, but was strongly suspected of handing over several of his comrades to the Gestapo.

At the same time that this information was complete,

there was evidence that Neukermanns was corresponding in code with addresses in neutral countries. He was arrested and tried at the Old Bailey before Mr. Justice MacNaughten. His defence was that he had come to Britain as a spy, but had been so impressed with what he saw that he had determined to disobey his German masters. The verdict was inevitable. He was executed in June 1944.

A month later another Belgian met his end at Pentonville after an Old Bailey trial before Mr. Justice Hallett. His name was Joseph Jan Vanhove, and he was in pre-war days a waiter. After the German occupation of Belgium he became a black marketeer, selling stolen Germany Army food on a commission basis. The Wermacht security police found out what was happening, the officer concerned was sent to the Russian front and Vanhove was thrown into prison. Black marketing was a capital offence, and the frightened little man was given the chance of saving his life by becoming a spy.

The scheme was a clever one. The German Secret Service announced that Vanhove had escaped. The Press of occupied Europe was ordered to publish details which indicated that the one-time waiter had been using his great and illegal fortune to finance resistance and sabotage. Overnight Vanhove became a hero of every patriot, and when in due course he turned up in Stockholm begging the British Embassy to take him to safety where he could resume the fight against Belgium's enemies he was in due course put on a transport plane for Britain. Vanhove was quite unworthy of the enormous trouble and expense the Germans went to in order to create the escape story that continued for months before their quarry reached the safety of Sweden. When he was arrested in London's dockland he had not managed to send a single worthwhile item of news to his masters.

The espionage cases heard during the Second World War, from a legal viewpoint usually of a cut-and-dried nature, aroused only minor interest compared with the trial of William Joyce in September 1945.

The case was of tremendous importance to the legal profession and to the public alike. The precise, delicately-enunciated words which had earned Joyce the title of Lord Haw Haw, when he introduced his vicious propaganda broadcasts with " This is Chairmany calling, Chairmany calling . . ." made it an intriguing thing to see the owner of this voice.

I think my own reaction to him was the general one. He looked as pathetically comic as the ridicule of his broadcasts had made him out to be. If this was an example of the Master Human whom Hitler was prepared to recruit from foreign lands to join his own Herrenvolk then he must indeed have been hard put to it to find allies.

Joyce's rather mild and mystified appearance was given an air of alarmed surprise by a gash which had been made by a razor in an affray between Fascists and Communists in the nineteen-twenties. He looked like a man of weak character but of terrific vanity.

But there was nothing comic and no flavour of the P. G. Wodehouse novel where Joyce seemed to belong when the charges were read out in the presence of the presiding Judge, Mr. Justice Tucker.

" First: Being a person owing allegiance to our Lord the King he adhered to the King's enemies elsewhere than in the King's Realm by broadcasting between September 18th, 1939, and May 29th, 1945.

" Second, that being a person owing allegiance to our Lord the King he adhered to the King's enemies elsewhere than in the King's Realm by purporting to become natural-ised in Germany.

" Third, being a person owing allegiance to our Lord the King he adhered to the King's enemies elsewhere than within the Realm by broadcasting between September 18th, 1939, and July 2nd, 1940."

Because of the decision that Joyce was of American birth, the Judge directed the jury to return a formal verdict of Not Guilty on the first two counts and the trial proceeded to decide the issue of the third count, the period concerned being one when Joyce held a British passport.

The problems before the Court were considerable. There was no precedent for this new form of treachery— the reaching out through the ether with words of alarm and despondency while the speaker sat in the security of the enemy capital and yet could drop his hints and spread his warnings in the very homes of his alleged compatriots whom he hoped to help destroy.

But more intricate was the answer to the ostensibly simple question: Who was Joyce?

He was born in Brooklyn, U.S.A., in 1906, the son of an Irish father and an English mother. Mr. Joyce, who incidentally died in England during the war, had become a naturalised American citizen years before his son was born. When William was three years old the family returned to Ireland, and in 1922, while the Irish troubles were at their height, they settled in England. No one, not even the local authorities, seem to have regarded them as aliens.

William, by now sixteen years of age, studied science at the Battersea Polytechnic, and then went on to Birkbeck College where he graduated. While there he joined the University of London O.T.C., insisting that he was a British subject, his father confirming this in writing.

It was at this time that William Joyce became enthusiastic about Fascism, and he spoke in support of it at political meetings. Not until 1933 did he make any attempt to go abroad and then, in applying for a passport, he called himself British and gave his country of birth as Ireland. It was on a renewal of this passport that he went off to Germany a day or two before war broke out. As soon as he could he became a German subject, but he had broadcast propaganda before then.

The tangle of nationality—actual, adopted, claimed, and rejected—was unravelled to the satisfaction of the jury, who deemed him guilty. Joyce appealed, claiming that he was an alien who had committed the alleged offence in a foreign country, that he owed no allegiance to the King, that he had never attempted to avail himself of the protection of his British passport, and that even if there was evidence that this protection was available because he was regarded as a British subject, the issue was one for the jury and there had been a failure on the Judge's part to direct them on this point.

The appeal failed. There was a further one a fortnight later to the House of Lords. That also failed, and Lord Haw Haw was executed on January 3, 1946, at Wandsworth Prison. There was one of the biggest crowds of recent times outside the gaol to read the usual notice that execution had been carried out.

It was a terrible end for a life which had, in its earlier years, promised much. But Joyce, who had once described Britain as " the country which I love so dearly ", was an evil man, ready to skulk in a heavily protected studio in Berlin and to gloat over the destruction of the country that had been his home and to vaunt about the truth of his prophecies that its peoples would be massacred if they dared to defend themselves.

The death of Joyce was, we hoped, the finale in the story of treachery and treason fertilised by the filth of war. Four months later another trial proved us wrong. Dr. Allan Nunn May stood in the dock while his Judge (Mr. Justice Oliver) heard the tawdry story of how he had passed on scientific secrets—and was paid two hundred dollars and a bottle of whisky for his trouble—to the Russian Intelligence Service. He pleaded guilty and was sentenced to ten years' penal servitude under the Official Secrets Act.

The case, as I recall it, created only slight public interest. There were vacant seats in the public gallery and no crowds outside. Perhaps it was too early to appreciate the real importance of the war-time developments in the field of nuclear fission. Many months were to pass before the full impact of the dangers of divided loyalties among scientists was revealed in the same Old Bailey Court where Dr. May had pleaded guilty.

The case I have in mind brought the most tragic scene I ever watched at the Old Bailey. It occurred at that dramatic pause in the proceedings between jury's verdict and Judge's sentence.

The man in the dock was silent for what cannot have been more than seconds even though it seemed an eternity. Then, in the precise, grammatical language of a person who has reached fluency in an adopted tongue after years of training and study, he quietly made his statement.

" My Lord," he said gently, " I have committed certain crimes for which I am charged and I expect sentence. I have also committed some other crimes which are not crimes in the eyes of the law—crimes against my friends. When I asked my counsel to put certain facts before you I did not do it because I wanted to lighten my sentence. I did it in order to atone for those other crimes. I have had a fair trial and I wish to thank your Lordship, my counsel, and my solicitors. I also wish to thank the Governor and staff of Brixton Prison for the considerate treatment they have given me."

These were the last words spoken in public by Emil Julius Klaus Fuchs, without doubt the greatest political criminal in history, for he altered the international scene, founded a new situation in the eternal war for power, and caused consternation in the chancelleries of a score of capitals. He had created a major world crisis with a dozen words spoken to a British security agent one afternoon in January 1950.

" I have told the Russians the method of making the atomic bomb," he confessed.

Never before have the world's eyes been focussed on an Old Bailey Court with such intensity as on March 1, 1950, when Fuchs was tried. I saw the Duchess of Kent, diplomatic representatives, famous foreign correspondents of the world's Press, scientists of the new Atomic Age, politicians whose faces were familiar, and military-looking men whose anonymity betrayed their importance, enter the

Old Bailey to watch the ancient precepts of British justice grapple with this new evil of twentieth century disquiet.

The Lord Chief Justice, Lord Goddard, heard the case. His scarlet and ermine garb, virtually identical with that of his predecessors in centuries past, the mediaeval pageantry of mace and sword-bearers, the quaint yet momentous legal phraseology which opened the proceedings and the serene quiet of the court room contrasted strangely with the bizarre world of modern science and the terrifying forces of ideology which had brought Klaus Emil Fuchs into that Court.

The trial lasted a mere ninety minutes. Legally it was a simple case. There was only one witness. Neither prosecution nor defence felt the need for histrionics. The Judge's summing up was masterly, but the very fact that Fuchs had pleaded guilty stripped much of the interest in it. Yet I am certain that the case will remain in the pages of history long after the murderers, the gangsters and the ordinary run of professional crooks have been forgotten.

Fuchs had the appearance of a man whose soul was already dead within him. Such utter mental desolation I have never seen as in the remote, faraway light of his eyes. He had long battled through the emotional crisis of his position, and reached some sort of hopeless coma which, if not peaceful, was at least a means of imposing control of his actions.

His face was pale, but not unnaturally so. His mouth, immobile and rigid, struck me as that of a kindly and sensitive man. No one could avoid being impressed by his splendid forehead—the sort of skull that would have delighted a Rodin. "You are looking at a second Einstein," an American journalist whispered to me, " one of humanity's greatest brains."

The specific charges against Fuchs concerned communication to unknown persons information which might have been useful to an enemy on four separate occasions: in Birmingham in 1943 ; in New York between December

1943 and August 1944 ; in Boston, Massachusetts, in February 1945 ; and in Berkshire in 1947.

Behind the inference of those statements that his activities were discovered lies an amazing story of modern espionage and counter-espionage.

Fuchs was born in Germany in December 1911, the son of a parson who, when Fuchs was fourteen, became a Quaker. Fuchs grew up in a country which suffered near-starvation, inflation and frightful unemployment during his most impressionable years. He himself went to Leipzig University, where he was active as a pacifist. Then, in 1931, in order to combat the growing Nazi influence among young people, he became a Communist. When Hitler came to power he fled to France. Tragedy beset his family. His mother and sister committed suicide ; his father was arrested by the Gestapo. In the autumn of 1933 Fuchs arrived, penniless and in utter despair, as a refugee in England.

For two years he lived as the guest of a kindly West Country Quaker family, becoming a research student at Bristol University. It was at this time that the German Consul there, obeying his Berlin masters to make German refugees' lives as unpleasant as possible, informed the local police that Fuchs was a member of the Communist Party. A routine check produced no evidence that Fuchs was taking part in any Communist activities in Bristol, and as every German refugee was branded a criminal, a Communist or a Jew by the Nazis, little notice was taken of the Consul's charge, beyond the fact that it helped to prove that the young man was not a Nazi Fifth Columnist.

Fuchs proved an unusually brilliant student. He rapidly attained degrees and was awarded scholarships, one of which took him to Edinburgh University, and there, in July 1939, he applied for naturalisation with his Professor's approval. The application was not heard before war was declared, when all such matters were shelved.

From May 1940 until January 1941 he was interned in Canada as an enemy alien. Back at Edinburgh University when he had been cleared of suspicion, he was invited in the late spring to help with some intricate mathematical problems being undertaken at Birmingham University.

And so Fuchs, in May 1941, signed the Official Secrets Act and started on work connected with the atomic bomb. Almost immediately, it is believed, he got in touch with a Russian agent and began to pass information. Not even the solemn oath of allegiance he made in August 1942, upon being granted British naturalisation, seems to have disturbed his conscience. Russia was a gallant ally of his newly adopted country, and he was determined to help her.

There were ruthless and unprincipled men in the intelligence sections of the Soviet Government who quickly realised that their eager stooge in Birmingham University not only was involved in some remarkable work but that he also had a marvellous brain which could analyse what was the objective. More and more urgent requests for information came to Fuchs, who passed on what he knew, sometimes in a house not far from Hyde Park, sometimes in a lonely road on the outskirts of Banbury, sometimes in cafés and at bus stops in Birmingham.

One of his contacts was a woman. It was to her that he imparted the news that he would be going to the United States to continue his work. The instructions given to him for developing his treacherous activities in New York were as bizarre as anything in a novel.

At a certain time every Saturday until contact was made he was to loiter around a street corner in the slum areas of East Side, New York, carrying a tennis ball in his hand. A man would approach carrying a book, wearing gloves, and carrying a second pair of gloves. He would identify himself as Raymond and together they would find a taxi and drive to a quiet restaurant. Raymond, incidentally, was in fact Harry Gold, now in an American gaol on a thirty years' sentence.

The meetings became regular, each time Fuchs providing some information. He was offered money but refused it, even when, in July 1944, he delivered the plans of the atomic bomb.

Shortly afterwards he went with the other scientists to the testing ground of Los Alamos, New Mexico, where security was so complete that contacts with Raymond, who had followed his fellow spy from New York, became most difficult. However, Fuchs could get out now and then to Santa Fe, and there the meetings were resumed. The last one, in September 1945, was to hand Raymond complete details of the test bomb, its construction, the method of detonation, and the effects of the explosion.

Before Fuchs returned to England arrangements were made for meeting fresh contacts in London. On the first Saturday of every month, at 8 p.m., he was to be at the entrance of a tube station in Central London, carrying five books tied up with string in one hand and two books in the other. The contact would be carrying an American joke book. Whether Fuchs kept this appointment is not certain. Probably the uncovering of the Canadian spy ring frightened both Fuchs and his contact, or there may have been a general order to all agents to lie low for a time. But by 1947 he was in contact again, and accepted £100 as a fee to cover his expenses. This, it is believed, was the first and last sum he ever had from his masters for information the value of which was incalculable. Fuchs was by this time an important personage at the Harwell research plant. He was well liked by his fellow scientists, and of course his brilliance ensured their respect and admiration. Unknown to any of the scientists, the security investigation had begun soon after Dr. Allan Nunn May had been arrested, tried and convicted in May 1946 ; the revelations in Canada indicated that in the heart of both the British and American atomic projects there were spies.

William Skardon, the only witness at Fuchs' trial, and one of the most brilliant servants of Britain's security forces, came to Harwell to assist the plant's security officer, Wing Commander Henry Arnold.

The actual questioning of Fuchs, based on irrefutable

evidence of his guilt privately known to Mr. Skardon, began in a quiet and friendly manner shortly before Christmas 1949. It continued at frequent intervals until January 24, 1950, when Fuchs finally decided to confess.

When he was formally arrested his comment was "You realise what this will mean at Harwell?"

It was the cry of a man who had grown to love his work and his adopted country, and now, when it was too late, to hate himself for his slavish adulation of Communism.

Perhaps, when he was waiting in the cells below the Old Bailey, he felt that there was nothing left to live for, and that in a way the settling of the whole sorry tangle of his career would be a blessed relief.

Shortly before the hearing I had seen Mr. Derek Curtis-Bennett, Fuchs' senior counsel, hurry to the cells in the basement for a last-minute conversation with his client. Lawyers have told me that the most painful task they have is to acquaint the prisoner with their honest opinion of the outcome of the trial—the invariable question that is asked—when the reply must be "There is not much hope."

Mr. Curtis-Bennett later stated that Fuchs took the news that in his counsel's opinion there was no chance of acquittal calmly enough—a reaction not unnatural in an intelligent man who had given a detailed and voluntary confession in an effort to make amends, but the calmness was remarkable because Fuchs wrongly believed that the punishment would be execution. As Russia was Britain's fighting ally when Fuchs began his activities he could not be hanged; the maximum penalty was fourteen years, which was what he received.

I had the impression that no punishment inflicted by his fellow men could match the hell which Fuchs had created in his own mind.

CHAPTER SEVEN

Women who faced the Brand of Cain

NO ONE WHO THEN WORKED AT THE OLD
Bailey will forget a December day in 1922. The almost
unbearable tension came when the jury had retired to
consider their verdict. It was a dismal and murky winter's
evening with a slight drizzle falling amidst the fog which
was illuminated by the gas lamps in the street.

I remember going to the doors of the Entrance Hall
and seeing the huge crowd which was being kept on the
move by the squads of police moving steadily up and down,
yet waiting like everybody inside the Court and out for the
verdict.

There was something almost horrible about that crowd
in the street because I had the impression that it was a
relic of the blood-hungry mob of previous centuries waiting
to gloat over those awful words " To be hanged by the
neck . . .".

At a quarter to six the jury filed back to their box in
the court room, which seemed by comparison with the
murk outside to be brightly illuminated. Everyone could
see from their white faces and the way that they avoided
looking at the man and woman in the dock that their
verdict would be the single word " Guilty " in both cases.
But it was the woman's reaction that everyone awaited.

Edith Thompson was held upright by two wardresses
while the dread sentence was pronounced on her. When
she had first come to the Old Bailey I had thought what
a pretty woman she was.

Yet in the short space of her trial she had become old
and ugly. Her face on that wintry night had literally
turned a grey colour. The hue was accentuated by the
enormous size of her staring eyes which seemed to grow
and grow as she took in what the Judge was saying. Her

delicate and shapely hands were gripping the rail in front of the dock so tightly that the bones stood out at the knuckles dead white in colour.

I do not think that she really heard the words of the Judge, Mr. Justice Shearman. As soon as the small black square had been placed on his head her eyes glazed over and she was virtually in a trance when the wardresses gently disengaged her fingers from the rail and half-carried her down the steps to the cells. It must have been the change of environment that forced into her numbed brain the awful truth. As always in a murder trial where the defendant has been found guilty there is a terrible silence lasting a few moments before the Judge rises and thereby permits the people in the Court to leave.

In those few moments after Edith Thompson had been taken below there came into the silent Court the wails of some stricken animal changing into inhuman shrieks of a human being. The terrible cries were almost unbearable as they became fainter and fainter while Edith Thompson was taken farther down the stone passage and at last the shutting of a cell door brought blessed silence to the court room.

In the uncanny way that news of this sort eddies outwards, the crowds in the streets quickly knew what the verdict had been. Their muttering became louder until the police cleared them away and the normal life of a city just finishing another working day brought back normality.

Without doubt this was the most memorable of all the charges of murder against a woman which I ever experienced during my fifty years at the Old Bailey. Her story showed the terrible tragedy which can come to an ordinary little suburban housewife who was possibly not destined by Fate to be a killer but through her foolish dreams and her offences against accepted codes of behaviour brought awful retribution from society.

Edith Graydon came from a neat little suburban home in Ilford. At school she had been rather a liar and somewhat secretive, but this was more than made up for by the fact that she was an outstandingly pretty girl and a highly intelligent one. It was her charm and ability that provided her with a secretarial job in the City. On the train to Liverpool Street which she took every morning, she often sat in the same compartment as a meek little clerk. From a casual nod and a smile they began to talk to one another and soon the friendship ripened into a romance.

Like tens of thousands of other young couples who meet on trains and buses going to work, they married and settled down in a small suburban house. The bridegroom's name was Percy Thompson. He was not a very exciting person, for his physique was so poor that he had been rejected for military service. While thousands of young wives would have given almost anything if their husbands had not been fit enough to be sacrificed to the god of war on the Western Front, Edith Thompson was secretly furious that her husband was not a soldier.

It was perhaps this failure of his that engendered in her mind the first traces of her contempt for him. He was, however, a man to be henpecked and he continued to adore and spoil his wife even though she insulted him and never failed to indicate her annoyance at his failure in practically everything that a man could fail in. Exasperated by the ease of her conquest over him, Edith turned more and more to a dream world, and day after day when Percy came home from his clerical activities in the City he found no meal ready, while his wife lay on a sofa in an untidy room reading the latest romantic novel from the lending library. The heroes of fiction seemed to assuage her yearning for thrills and romance, until just after the war when she went on holiday with her husband to the Isle of Wight.

There in a cheap boarding house she became friendly with another person from Ilford, a handsome youth of nineteen named Frederick Bywaters. Edith was at that time twenty-seven years of age. She built him up into a far more romantic figure than in actual fact he was. But

Bywaters could at least provide her with exciting stories of the world because he was a liner steward. The holiday in the Isle of Wight was only of a fortnight's duration, but before Edith returned home with her husband she had persuaded Frederick to give her a schedule of the ports at which his ship would call on its passage from Southampton to Australia.

The vessel was not leaving for some days, and this enabled Edith to start the torrent of passionate letters which were read during the hearing of the murder case. At every port at which the liner called another effusion was awaiting her young lover.

It was not unnatural that a youth of nineteen was greatly flattered by all that he read in Edith's letters, and the result was that when his ship returned to England they became lovers in reality.

Still Edith was dissatisfied because Frederick seemed to be a very poor imitation of the sheiks and millionaires which were the heroes of her interminable supply of romantic novels. In an effort to arouse her lover's jealousy she used to tell him the most hair-raising stories of the cruelties which her husband inflicted on her. Every story was a tissue of lies but they had the desired effect of increasing the young man's infatuation for her to the extent that he half-heartedly agreed to help her poison Percy Thompson.

She seemed to think that it would be easy for him to purchase mysterious and untraceable poisons in practically any Asiatic port that he visited, and when he returned from his next voyage empty-handed she was furious with him. She herself pretended that she had tried all sorts of poisons herself and claimed that she had pounded an electric lamp to small pieces and fed it to her husband as a powder sprinkled among the sugar on his breakfast porridge. This incidentally was pure imagination, for no trace of powdered glass in Percy Thompson's body was found after his death.

The tirade of confessions and exhortations had their effect. Young Frederick Bywaters became intensely jealous.

He believed implicitly that it was his destiny to destroy his rival. At a meeting of the lovers in October 1922, Edith told Frederick that her husband was going to take her out to a dinner and theatre in the West End. Somehow she glossed over the fact that this kindness on his part hardly tallied with all her stories of his diabolical treatment of her.

Whether the two of them then carefully planned the frightful attack which resulted will never be known. Perhaps it was Edith Thompson's fertile brain that devised every act of the tragedy that occurred, perhaps she allowed the seeds of hatred to germinate in Frederick's mind so that he planned it all himself. What did happen was that close on midnight husband and wife were walking arm-in-arm through the deserted streets of Ilford to their home. Suddenly in a quiet avenue of small residential houses Frederick lunged out from the shadows and hurled himself on Percy Thompson, slashing him again and again with a knife.

The man's frenzy seemed to have given him superhuman strength, and so vicious was one thrust that it laid the victim's spinal column bare. The second slash went right through from the back of the neck to the interior of the mouth, and a third cut the main artery in the gullet. Percy Thompson collapsed in the gutter and made frightful noises from his mutilated mouth and throat in the few seconds that were left to him before he died.

There was a woman going to bed in a house just opposite the scene of the attack who said that she heard Edith Thompson cry out " Don't, don't! " Other residents heard the noise and went outside. One of them called a doctor.

There was, of course, nothing that he could do, and as he laid a handkerchief over the dead man's face Edith Thompson clawed hysterically at him crying: " Why didn't you come sooner and save him? " And then, as if already taking refuge in her imagination, added: " If you will allow him to be taken home I will make him better."

A woman comforted her and took her into her house, telling her that she must realise how fortunate she was that she had not also been the victim of some maniac killer who was obviously abroad that night.

Of the assailant there was no trace at all, but it took the police very little time to discover the facts about Mrs. Thompson's intrigue, and Bywaters was rapidly found and detained for questioning. By accident Mrs. Thompson saw him sitting in a room when she walked down the corridor of the police station.

" Oh God, oh God," she cried, " What can I do, why did he do it, I didn't want him to do it, I must tell the truth."

This hysterical outburst did, of course, sign the death warrant of Frederick Bywaters and at the same time implicated her in the crime. It must be said in Bywaters' favour that he said over and over again that Edith was quite ignorant of the crime and an innocent party to it. But her sixty letters, many of which contained plans for getting rid of her husband, reports on her efforts to kill him herself, and pleas that her lover should kill him next time he came home, inevitably meant that she had to stand trial for murder as well.

The question of the degree of Edith Thompson's guilt has, of course, interested the legal profession ever since her conviction. For me, whether she was a cold-blooded and calculating conspirator in a murder plot, or an hysterical and imaginative woman who unleashed devilish powers which she neither wished to curb nor was capable of controlling, are unanswerable questions.

There is another murder case in my memory with a woman defendant, which for the major part of the time at least was just as harrowing as that of Edith Thompson. This was the trial of Ethel Le Neve, Dr. Crippen's lover. Crippen was sentenced to death, after his case had lasted a whole week, as I describe in Chapter Four, on October 22, 1910.

Three days later Ethel Le Neve was charged with being an accessory to murder after the fact. The modern generation can have no conception whatever of the notoriety of this quiet and unassuming little typist at this time. Her liaison with the murderer, her effort to escape with him to America after going to Rotterdam where she cut off her hair and was dressed as a boy, posing as Dr. Crippen's son, the almost noble insistence of Crippen at every stage of his trial of her complete innocence, and the strong suspicion aroused during the evidence at that trial that she must have at least been aware of the crime, even if she was not an accomplice, made her case not an anti-climax to the drama of three days before, but yet another instalment of horror.

The presiding judge was Lord Alverstone and she was defended by the famous F. E. Smith (later Lord Birkenhead). I think that the majority of the staff of the Old Bailey felt certain that she would be found guilty, and even if she was not hanged would be imprisoned for life. The circumstantial evidence was strong.

In the first place there were the guilty relations between the two which had been, so far as was known, the sole motive for Dr. Crippen's wishing to get rid of his wife. There were witnesses who said that immediately after the presumed date of the victim's death, Ethel Le Neve had become extremely ill as if she were overcome by profound remorse.

The gentleness of her character and the placidity of her face as she stood in the dock seemed to be misleading when the evidence proved that within a day or two of the murder she was attending social functions with her lover, wearing the dead woman's jewellery.

She went openly to live at the house where the paving in the cellar, under which Mrs. Crippen's mutilated body had been buried, must still have shown devious signs of disturbance. After she fled with her lover to Holland the newspapers of the world were packed with details of the crime discovered in the basement of the ominous house in Hilldrop Crescent.

It was difficult to believe that she had neither seen a single headline nor read a single paragraph of the spate of news which was poured out at the time when she was being fitted with boys' clothes. But thanks to a brilliant defence, it was soon evident that it would have to be a most unusual jury to convict her.

The Judge's summing up left little doubt as to the verdict he thought the jury should return, and in the event they quickly gave one of " Not Guilty ".

Ethel Le Neve was a tiny person, pretty in a rather wan sort of way, and I think that from my own study of her as she patiently listened to the forensic brilliance of both prosecution and defence, she felt a submissiveness to fate. It was indeed difficult to believe that this young woman who was really so ordinary of face and so quiet in behaviour and appearance engendered one of the greatest loves of modern times.

In his last statement for publication, Dr. Crippen said: " In this farewell letter to the world written as I face eternity, I say that Ethel Le Neve has loved me as few women love men."

After insisting that she was innocent of any crime or complicity in any crime, he added: " To her I pay this last tribute. It is of her that my last thoughts have been. My last prayer will be that God will protect her and keep her safe from harm and allow her to join me in eternity."

Her letters to him, her photograph, the farewell telegram which she sent to him at Pentonville Prison, were buried with him. Compliance with requests of this kind from convicted murderers are rare and it is perhaps a testimony to the strange power of this girl's love that authority unbent on this occasion. And I know that I along with others whose duty it was to assist the awful processes of the law, succumbed in some strange way to this girl's personality, so that I was relieved when she stepped from the dock a free woman—eventually to go to Australia and be lost in oblivion until her reported death after the last war, her secret of how much she really knew—or how little she knew—of her lover's terrible crime going to the grave with her.

Another triangle murder case in which a woman

endured the limelight of the Old Bailey on a murder charge was that of Alma Rattenbury, tried with George Stoner. I shall long remember it because a Nemesis far more terrible than the punishment of man-made justice brought eventual tragedy. Before the strain of the police investigation coming on top of a life in which she had indulged in many excesses, I can well believe that Alma Rattenbury must have been a very beautiful woman. Even in the last few weeks of her life she looked far younger than her thirty-eight years. Mrs. Rattenbury and Stoner were tried at the Old Bailey in May 1935, before Mr. Justice Humphreys.

The story revealed at the trial was a terrible exposure of the sort of thing that can go on in a quiet domestic house in England.

Francis Rattenbury, an architect in Canada, had been divorced in 1928 and married the woman in the case, Alma. He was then in his late fifties and his bride a woman of thirty. A child was born of the marriage and thereafter the couple ceased to live as man and wife. They were, however, ostensibly quite happy and Rattenbury certainly wanted nothing more than companionship, whatever frustration his wife may have felt.

He was a generous man and allowed her a housekeeping budget of £1,000 a year, which was more than sufficient for their pleasant but modest little home in Bournemouth called the " Villa Madeira ". Two servants were originally employed, and after one of them left husband and wife agreed that it might be a good idea to engage a boy or young man who could combine the heavy jobs inside the house with a bit of gardening and looking after the car.

They advertised in the local Press for a " Daily Boy " aged fourteen to eighteen, and as a result George Stoner, seventeen years of age, applied. Both his prospective employers liked him and on being engaged for the post he proved a willing worker—so much so that they suggested that he might prefer to live in. Within a matter of days Mrs. Rattenbury and George Stoner were lovers.

Whether Mr. Rattenbury suspected what was going on or not will never be known. It seems unlikely that in such a small household he could have been totally unaware of the situation, for the evidence indicated that the lovers were very indiscreet, and it is more than probable that he was ready to acquiesce in it. On the other hand, Mrs. Rattenbury gave the impression to most visitors to her home that her affection was mostly maternal. She worked hard to correct Stoner's speech, to teach him proper manners and to educate him.

The household lived quite amicably until the early spring of 1935 when an exceptionally fine period of weather tempted Mr. and Mrs. Rattenbury to drive down to Dorset to visit some friends for the weekend. Stoner overheard this conversation and took the first opportunity of way-laying his mistress and warning her " I will kill you if you go on that trip."

Alma Rattenbury took no notice of the remark, for it was not the first time that he had made moody threats through the pangs of jealousy. But at 11 o'clock that night the maid in the house was aroused by Mrs. Rattenbury screaming.

The girl hurried downstairs and found her mistress in her pyjamas crying: " Oh poor Ratz, what have they done to you? "

Mrs. Rattenbury was stooping over a big armchair in which her husband sat with his head tilted back as if he were asleep. One eye was bruised and on the floor by the side of the chair was a pool of blood. The three deep wounds at the back of his skull were hidden by the back of the chair.

Stoner was called. He came downstairs and was sent to get the car out to fetch the doctor, for whom the maid was already telephoning.

It was three days before Francis Rattenbury died and in that time he did not regain consciousness. As soon as the doctor had seen the nature of the wounds he telephoned for the police. When they arrived they found the house blazing with light, the radio-gramophone blaring dance music and Alma Rattenbury walking up and down the room with a tumbler of whisky in her hand.

She was in an advanced state of drunken hysteria and the police officers could make little of what she was saying beyond the fact that there had been an armed intruder— information which was soon contradicted by her by claiming that she had herself struck her husband.

After an hour of looking for clues and trying to get a statement from her, during which time her hysteria gave way to complete drunkenness so that she was laughing and singing, and now and then trying to kiss the officers, they left her alone until the following morning.

She then insisted that she had struck her husband, and there was nothing to be done but formally charge her with intent to murder. Her friends were horrified at what they regarded as the obtuseness of the police and they insisted that she was the type of woman who was incapable of hurting a fly.

The police took note of this evidence because they themselves already recognised that a brutal attack with some kind of axe was quite uncharacteristic of a female murderer, and when the maid told them of her suspicions as regards Mrs. Rattenbury's love affair with the allegedly model servant, Stoner, they arrested him.

Until then he had continued quietly living in the house, going about his daily jobs and being so self-effacing that he had hardly been noticed. As soon as he was in custody his first remark was: " Do you know that Mrs. Rattenbury had nothing to do with the affair? "

This attempt to shoulder all the blame himself which was paralleled by Mrs. Rattenbury's endeavour to do the same in order to allow Stoner to go free, was an almost unique example in a murder case of two lovers fighting with all their might to take all the blame, irrespective of the facts.

But in the three day trial before Mr. Justice Humphreys, it was soon quite evident that Mrs. Rattenbury had been quite unaware of the assault on her husband until a noise brought her downstairs. The jury retired for forty-seven minutes. The verdict on the charge against Mrs. Rattenbury was given first. She stood immovable when the foreman of the jury said " Not Guilty ", but she moaned and tried to reach out to her lover with her hand when a minute later George Stoner was found guilty of murder. She had to wait while another indictment against her was discussed—that of being an accessory after the fact—and by then she was too numbed to be aware of what was going on, because when the Clerk of the Court asked her whether she was " Guilty " or " Not Guilty " there was no sound at all, merely a twitching of the lips which in the mercy of the Court was naturally taken as her version of " Not Guilty ".

No evidence was offered on this indictment and she was then discharged.

She was smuggled out of the Court in an attempt to enable her to avoid the hordes of journalists who wanted to obtain an interview with her.

The reaction came soon afterwards and she had to go into a nursing home. Somehow or other she managed to get out, reach Waterloo and take the train to Bournemouth. There she walked out into the countryside until she came to a little stream where she sat down and tried to write her thoughts on paper. They were incoherent messages making little sense. Then she took hold of a small knife and plunged it into her breast. She managed what most doctors would consider the impossible feat of repeating the thrusts six times, on three of them penetrating the heart. Her body was found soon afterwards by a farmworker.

Three weeks later Stoner was reprieved. Fate in her infinite wisdom had taken away the life of the woman whom man had decreed to be guiltless and given it back to the man that society had condemned to death.

It is always a difficult and exciting time for those who work at the Old Bailey when a notorious murder trial occurs. It becomes even more troublesome when the defendant is a woman.

If she is, for some reason, well-known or notorious in her own right, then the treasured privilege that justice must be done in open Court, to which all the Monarch's subjects must be admitted without let or hindrance, becomes strained to the very limit.

One case in my memories which more than fulfilled all these provisions was that of Mrs. Elvira Barney in 1932. She was described by the famous barrister who defended her, Sir Patrick Hastings, as a spoilt child of fortune. This summed her up perfectly. She was the daughter of titled parents and from childhood had been accustomed to every form of luxury and comfort that money could purchase. It was a foregone conclusion from the preliminary hearings of her case that the Old Bailey trial before Mr. Justice Humphreys would be one of the major sensations of the year.

When I arrived at work that morning Newgate Street and Holborn were crammed with parked limousines. Outside the entrance to No. 1 Court fashionably dressed women and men whom one would have expected to be in the Directors' room of some City company by that time were queuing with the usual ragged and motley crowd that makes a fetish of attending any and every trial.

Inside the building more privileged persons, including friends of the legal personalities concerned in the case, famous authors and artists who had been engaged at high fees by the Press, were waiting avidly for what it was universally believed would be the official branding of yet another woman with the mark of Cain. From the outset the case had gained enormous publicity because of its revelations of the behaviour of the so-called " Mayfair Set ".

Mrs. Barney was married, but she had been separated from her husband for some time. Fundamentally unhappy and with nothing to do but plenty of money with which to try to amuse herself, she had drifted into a life which consisted principally of visiting night-clubs and attending wild parties. It was at one of these parties that she got to know a worthless young man named Stephens. He called himself a dress designer but in fact he had no occupation and no resources. Mrs. Barney rented a flat above a garage in a Knightsbridge mews and there set up house with him. Their neighbours heartily disliked the couple because of the noise in the flat either when they were quarrelling or on the occasion of the numerous hectic parties which they gave.

It was shortly after midnight that a nearby doctor received a telephone call from Mrs. Barney. When he lifted the receiver she was crying out in hysteria: " Doctor, come at once! There has been an accident. For God's sake come! "

The doctor went round immediately and saw the man Stephens lying at the top of the narrow stairs from the entrance in the mews to the flat. He was dead.

Mrs. Barney was sitting on the top stairs caressing the man's head and trying to pretend that he was still alive. Lying beside her was a revolver.

The police were called, and the story that Mrs. Barney told them was that she had quarrelled with Stephens because he threatened to leave her. She had tried to make him change his mind by saying that she would commit suicide. To convince him that she meant what she said she crossed to the bedside table and from a drawer took out a revolver. He came across and tried to grab it from her. The gun went off and Stephens staggered through the doorway, falling as he tried to go down the stairs.

The story seemed reasonable and after Mrs. Barney had visited the local police station and given some further details, her parents were called and she was allowed to go to their home.

Early next morning detectives began to question neighbours who lived in the mews and from them they obtained a somewhat different story. A woman neighbour said that she had heard the couple quarrelling and insisted that during the altercation more than one shot was fired.

Another neighbour swore that she had clearly heard Mrs. Barney saying: " I will shoot you."

Yet another witness alleged that in an earlier quarrel they had seen Stephens walking down the narrow street while Mrs. Barney, leaning out of the window of the flat, shouted after him: " Laugh, baby; laugh for the last time." She then took a shot at him. Naturally with evidence of this kind the police attitude to Mrs. Barney was immediately altered. She was arrested and charged with murder.

It was obvious that with Sir Patrick Hastings to defend her and expert witnesses for the prosecution like Sir Bernard Spilsbury and Mr. Churchill, the firearms expert, the case was going to be a historic legal battle. I must confess that it was with some eagerness that I waited to see the famous Elvira Barney arrive, half expecting to see a really lovely young woman.

The photographs which the Press had obtained were studio portraits and the actual sight of the prisoner was extremely disappointing. The photographs had obviously been taken some years before and although she was still a young woman, time had dealt hardly with her. It was perhaps to her ultimate benefit that she was not the brittle and vivacious social butterfly which Press stories had led everybody to expect. English juries are very conventional in their outlook and the quiet and rather melancholy woman who stood in the dock undoubtedly produced more sympathy in their minds than the journalistic version would have done.

Although Sir Patrick Hastings fought brilliantly, particularly in a clash with Sir Bernard Spilsbury, it was really Mrs. Barney herself who achieved the triumph. When she went into the witness box she gave her evidence calmly and objectively. It was a rather disgusting story of a wasted life that she had to tell but she made no attempt to hide anything. It was perfectly obvious to everybody that when she said over and over again as the reason for some silly action that she felt so unhappy, everybody could believe her. Gradually the picture appeared of the worthless and callous young man who had been her lover and the victim in the shooting incident.

Under cross-examination she did not waver one bit from her story that all her actions with the gun had been either to frighten her lover and make him return to her, or, on one or two occasions, to try to commit suicide.

The damning evidence of the neighbours was changed bit by bit. For example the allegation that Mrs. Barney had been heard to say: " I will shoot you " was rebutted with an admission that it might have been: " I will shoot ".

Her bitter challenge to Stephens to suggest that he should laugh for the last time could quite easily be the final words of a woman determined to end her own life. Yet when the jury retired it was still a perfectly open question as to what their verdict would be.

I managed to get into the crowded Court when the word went round that the jury was about to return. Mrs. Barney had been brought back and she stood very white and yet very calm beside the wardress. The jury filed in and I saw one or two of them glance quite openly in the defendant's direction.

There was no need to wonder any more what their verdict would be. An audible sigh of relief went round the quiet court and the Clerk rose to ask the time-honoured question. It was a foregone conclusion that Mrs. Barney was about to leave the Old Bailey a free woman.

CHAPTER EIGHT

The Mania of Murder

ONE OF THE MOST USUAL QUESTIONS WHICH friends and acquaintances put to me is: "What does the murderer look like?"

Whenever I have been asked this in recent years my thoughts turn to an autumn day in 1946 when, in No. 1 Court at the Old Bailey, I looked at a handsome 29-year-old man, fair-haired and blue-eyed, with a strong jaw and a not unkindly mouth. He looked like the typical young man you would see any Saturday afternoon on the football pitches or cricket fields of England. He had, indeed, that air of command and boldness which typified those who had followed his own profession during the war—that of an R.A.F. pilot.

I am quite certain that on the strength of his appearance (even if later one's suspicions were aroused by his rather brash manner and cocky conversation) no one who had met this young man in an hotel or a night club would have considered him anything but utterly charming; this feeling would have applied all the more strongly in the case of any woman who met him. Yet this man who had sat in court with an emotionless face for a total of fifteen hours was probably the most revolting murderer of the century.

His name was Neville George Clevely Heath. Even the Old Bailey, in which the horrors of centuries of human viciousness have been recorded, must never have been the scene of such revelations of such bestiality before. The trial was before Mr. Justice Morris, and Heath was defended by Mr. J. D. Casswell, K.C., Mr. E. A. Jessel and Mr. J. MacGillivray Asher.

He was charged with the murder of Margery Gardner at a Bayswater hotel. It was known that he had also killed Doreen Marshall and that he had attacked a third woman, but no evidence in this regard was offered.

THE GUILTY AND THE INNOCENT

As the story of his crime was unfolded during the three-day hearing, no one could have had any doubt that he was guilty, and the whole matter hinged on whether he was insane. By all normal decent human standards he must have been morally decadent, but as the Judge told the jury " the law of insanity is not to become a refuge to those who cannot challenge a charge brought against them ".

The jury, which consisted of ten men and two women, retired when the clock in the Old Bailey pointed to 4.35. They returned almost exactly one hour later, when the Foreman answered the Clerk's usual question with: " Guilty, the verdict of us all."

It was when asked whether he had anything to say why sentence of death should not be passed according to the law that Heath uttered the fourth word he had said during the whole trial. " Nothing ", he answered, clearly and firmly.

After the Judge, whose face was almost grey with fatigue and emotion, had pronounced sentence, Neville Heath stood up and walked erect and strangely proud to the steps which led to the cells below, and soon afterwards the prison van drove out of the Old Bailey on the way to Pentonville Prison.

So ended what I can truthfully say was the most upsetting trial during my years at the Old Bailey. The reason for the feeling of revulsion and dread which, I think, permeated the minds of everyone in that Court was that Heath seemed ostensibly so normal, and one had deep forebodings that only by a hair's breadth did other seemingly decent and pleasant young men escape from the awful sexual sadism which, at times, makes man lower than any animal that walks or crawls on the face of the earth.

As an essay in police detection, or as an example of a legal battle, the Heath case is of no importance. It is a red-lettered story in the calendar of crime, simply because of its terrible revelations of human vileness.

The murder for which Heath was hanged took place in the early hours of June 21, 1946, when Heath escorted a woman, Margery Gardner, he had met at a dance club in

Frederick Bywaters arriving at Ilford Court for the inquest, 1922

Crowds outside the Old Bailey await the result of the Thompson-
Bywaters trial

Edith Thompson—murderess   Elvira Barney—innocent

Horatio Bottomley, self-styled Friend of the Poor, is brought to
Bow Street, 1921

Dr. Crippen   John George Haigh

Neville George Clevely Heath   John Reginald Halliday Christie

Christie and the Notting Hill murders: the back garden of
No. 10 Rillington Place, where police dug for remains of victims

South Kensington to the hotel where Heath had stayed before.

He had booked a double room for the night in question, and had been given the front door key so that he was able to enter without being seen.

None of the other guests nor the staff seem to have heard anything amiss during the night, and it was not until the following afternoon that a chamber-maid, who had knocked at intervals, decided to open the door.

The curtains were drawn. All she was able to do was to make out the silhouette of a figure under the bedclothes in one of the twin beds. The very stillness of that figure aroused her suspicions and she drew the curtains. It was then that she saw the woman was dead.

The description of the injuries Mrs. Gardner had sustained were undoubtedly the most terrible I have ever heard in a court of law. Most of the details are unprintable, but it can be said that her ankles were fastened together, one arm had been tied to her body, and her torso had been lashed with a frenzy of sub-human strength. The medical evidence given at the trial indicated that the frightful internal and external injuries which had been inflicted on her had been produced before death and that Mrs. Gardner had, in fact, died from suffocation.

Hours before that tragic room had been entered by the chamber-maid, Heath had arrived in Worthing. He had left the hotel before anyone was up and had taken an early train to Brighton, the reason being that he had an appointment with a young lady with whom he had also spent a night at the hotel under the promise of marriage a few days before.

It might be mentioned that this girl, who had to undergo the terrible embarrassment of giving evidence about her love affair during the trial, was able to say that Heath had been a perfectly normal and affectionate man towards her.

He seemed to be in excellent spirits when he phoned her at her home and at lunch in a Worthing hotel he was his usual charming self. On the following day the newspapers were full of details of the body that had been found in the hotel and Heath went out of his way to mention to the girl that it had been found in the bedroom they had shared. He said that he knew something about the girl and would tell her when they met again that evening.

Before that meeting Heath was introduced to the girl's parents for she herself was convinced that she would soon be married to him. When the young couple went to a dinner and dance that evening Heath again referred to the murder and said that he had given the key of the bedroom to a man friend of his who was proposing to take a woman there, and he added that in his opinion the crime was obviously the work of a sexual maniac. Apart from a short phone call early the next morning this was the last that the girl saw of Heath until he was standing in the dock, which was perhaps as well for her.

Heath next decided to write a letter to Scotland Yard. Admittedly he had to do something because his name had come up in connection with the death in the hotel bedroom and he was by this time a person "that the police considered might be able to assist in their enquiries".

The purport of this letter was that he had given the key to Mrs. Gardner who had told him that she intended to sleep with a person unnamed during the early part of the night and that he, Heath, if he required to use the room later would find her alone after 2 a.m.

He went on to say that he returned at 3 a.m., found her dead, and realising that his position was serious decided to run off without informing the police. He gave a description of the man whom, he alleged, Mrs. Gardner had been seeing and added that he had the whip with which the woman had been beaten.

His next stopping place was the Tollard Royal Hotel at Bournemouth where he signed the register as Group Captain Rupert Brooke. After ten days or so he made the acquaintance of Doreen Marshall, a girl from Pinner, Middlesex, who was convalescing from illness at an hotel very close to Heath's. He invited her to tea and dinner at his hotel and afterwards they sat in the lounge until midnight. They left together to walk back to Miss Marshall's hotel. That was the last that was ever seen of her alive.

Two days after her disappearance, the manager of the hotel at which Miss Marshall had been staying started to make enquiries. He rang his colleague at the Tollard Royal saying that he believed his guest had taken dinner with a man there. The man questioned Heath, who denied that the girl he had spent the evening with was Miss Marshall, but he seemed to agree to the manager's suggestion that he should get in touch with the police.

Five days after Doreen Marshall had disappeared a lady was exercising her dog around Branksome Chine in the evening. The dog went off the path and seemed to be excited about something in the rhododendron bushes, and the animal's owner noticed that there was an abnormal number of flies around. She returned home, told her father, and both of them went to investigate. There they found the body of Doreen Marshall covered by her clothing and a few twigs and small branches. The police were immediately informed and in the vicinity they found various possessions of the girl's, including a broken pearl necklace, her handbag and her stockings.

Medical evidence indicated that the cause of death was a wound in the throat. The hands were lacerated as if the victim had attempted to pull the blade of a knife from the hands of her assailant. Her chest had been crushed with such violence that a rib had splintered and pierced the lung. The terrible and unprintable mutilations which had been inflicted on the corpse after death were very similar to those which Margery Gardner had suffered.

Before the discovery of this body Heath had been receiving the close attention of the Bournemouth police. He had been compelled to admit that he had known Doreen Marshall and that she had indeed been his guest on the night she disappeared.

At the interview it was noticed that he had scratches on

his neck and one of the detectives had a growing suspicion that he closely resembled the man whom Scotland Yard wished to interview in connection with the Bayswater murder. He was challenged with this and denied it vehemently.

Nevertheless the police felt that he should be detained pending further enquiries and as he had arrived in a sports shirt and trousers he asked if someone might be sent to get his jacket from the hotel.

The detective who went to get it looked in the pockets and there he found a cloakroom ticket issued from Bournemouth West railway station. With this ticket a suitcase was taken from the cloakroom. It contained a blood-stained scarf and a riding whip, of which the thongs had worn away at the ends, so that the wire base was exposed. Also in the pockets of the jacket was a return half of a ticket from Bournemouth to London which was later proved to have belonged to Doreen Marshall. A pearl which matched exactly those which had been found in the broken necklace near her body completed the ominous array of clues from this part of the investigations.

That night Heath volunteered to make a statement and he wrote continuously for more than three hours. He was by now no longer pretending to be Group Captain Rupert Brooke, but admitted that his name was Neville Heath. The first part of his statement was a fairly specious explanation of his meeting with Doreen Marshall and of circumstantial evidence designed to prove that he had left her long before the murder had taken place. He hinted that there was an American boy friend or two and that her insistence that he should not accompany her all the way to the hotel indicated that she had some kind of assignation. However, all of this statement was designed to clear him of any guilt of the murder of Doreen Marshall and he made no reference to the Bayswater killing.

The next morning a detective arrived from Scotland Yard and in due course Heath was charged with the murder of Margery Gardner. His reply was that he had nothing to say. Such was the tragic climax of Heath's life which brought him to the Old Bailey and thence to the gallows.

Behind this frightful story of his last few days as an ostensibly normal citizen was a background which seemed to lead inevitably to a disastrous end. As a child he had shown dishonest tendencies, more marked than those of the normally mischievous young boy.

At the infants' school that he attended in Ilford he was known as a precocious, resourceful little liar. By the time he was ten, he had the habit of stealing minor possessions of his fellow pupils and the teachers—notably handkerchiefs, a fetish which remained with him until the end. He was, however, quite a clever boy and he did well at school with his lessons and even better in sport. He was a first-class athlete and won a large number of prizes.

His first job after he left school was as a clerk with a firm of wholesale drapers in St. Paul's Churchyard. He also joined the Artists Rifles which gave him access, even though his wages were only £1 a week, into clubs where he got to know wealthy and socially important people.

In February 1936 he joined the R.A.F. on a short service commission, but in a little over a year he was court-martialled for being absent without leave for four months. This seemed to be the beginning of a career of minor crime. He borrowed money where he could and never paid it back. He stayed at hotels and left without paying the bill. He obtained a car on hire purchase and then sold it. When he was caught he got off with probation as a first offender and almost immediately took up robbery as a source of income to meet his expensive tastes. This brought him a sentence of three years in Borstal, but he was released on the outbreak of war and despite his prison record and the R.A.F. court martial he was able to obtain a commission in the R.A.S.C., whereupon he was posted to the Middle East. The usual story of dishonoured cheques, borrowed money and fraud upon his fellow-officers brought another court martial and he was cashiered.

He next turned up in South Africa where he enlisted in

117

the Air Force under the name of Armstrong. Once again the remarkable slackness of the armed forces in selecting their officers stood him in good stead. Even though it was quickly discovered that he in reality was the twice court-martialled Neville Heath, he was granted a commission because he was an excellent pilot. Even though at that time he was under a cloud for the usual financial frauds, nothing was done to curb his career, and by February 1944 he was back with the U.K. R.A.F. and flew with a bomber squadron until his aircraft was damaged and he had to bail out during the attacks on the flying-bomb sites in North-west France.

The notable events during the next twelve months were that the wife he had taken while in South Africa had divorced him for desertion and he was again court-martialled for wearing decorations without authority and on the all-embracing charge of conduct prejudicial to good order and discipline.

From that time until he was arrested for murder he appears to have had no job, managing to live by borrowing money where he could, battening on the numerous wealthy friends whom he could always captivate with his charm and indulging in a few little deals in the black market which presented such a ready source of money at that time.

The story of his life might be summed up as that of a " bad boy "—which is the usual rather tolerant attitude of people to a likeable man who, whatever people said about him, was good-looking, courageous and always ready to be a " good sport ".

Perhaps the strangest thing about Heath is that although any woman who attracted him was clearly in the most awful danger from his perverted sexuality, women did like him and many with whom he had love affairs could tell of nothing abnormal in his behaviour. The wife who divorced him in South Africa for desertion had no complaint to make beyond that she was a spurned woman and that he seemed to have no interest whatever in the child that she had borne him.

The wealthy girl in South Africa to whom he proposed as soon as his divorce came through regarded him as a most likeable and honourable person. The young lady at Worthing who sat starry-eyed at lunch a matter of hours after he had committed his first murder could not, on oath in Court, say anything repellent about his love-making.

It seemed to me that Heath was basically a terribly normal young man, part devil and part angel, but the devil in him was released with diabolical results.

While I watched Neville Heath in the box, my mind went back over the years to another famous murder case in which the prisoner's background bore uncannily parallels and similarities.

This was the Ronald True murder trial of 1922. During that hearing there was no evidence producing such blatant horror as in the case of the Heath trial, but at the same time I think that the bizarre details of the prisoner's life that emerged gave an even stronger feeling of disquiet about the strangeness of human behaviour. The most remarkable rumours circulated at the time that True was the illegitimate son of a very well-known woman. Some people said that she was of Royal blood, while almost all stories insisted that she was a member of one of the oldest and most aristocratic families of the country.

There is no point at this stage of reviving the controversy except to say that Ronald True's mother was by no means so illustrious as the stories suggested, although she came from a wealthy family. The baby was in fact born in Manchester in 1891, when his mother was only sixteen years of age. No suggestion can be made that the tragedies of his later life were due to any maltreatment in infancy and childhood because of his illegitimacy. In fact, Ronald was most carefully brought up. When he was ten years of age his mother married and her husband was human and decent enough to see that his wife's son had every possible advantage of education and care.

The last years of Ronald True's education were at Bedford Grammar School where he struggled on as a rather poor scholar until he was eighteen. He was then a mentally lazy but physically fine specimen of young manhood, and it was at his own wish as much as through any pressure on the part of his stepfather that he went to New Zealand to learn farming. True never liked hard work and he left the farm after a few months, and eventually arrived in the Argentine. There he secured a job on a ranch on the strength of his boastings of his experience in New Zealand, but he was, of course, soon revealed as absolutely incompetent.

Off he went to Canada where he joined the North-west Mounted Police, but that famous force soon had very little time for him or he for them.

On the outbreak of the First World War he was in Shanghai. The news of the hostilities in France thrilled him and he rushed to England where, despite the fact that there were a number of blots on his past career, and he was a drug addict, he was able to join the Royal Flying Corps as an officer cadet.

It was at this juncture that the parallel with Heath becomes so remarkably strong. Both men seemed to have been accepted by the service authorities without any serious investigation of their character or past record and both evidently gave a superficial impression that they were the fearless, devil-may-care type which makes a good airman. Heath, it must be admitted, did on occasions show some of that quiet courage while deliberately facing danger in flying over enemy territory that is the mark of real bravery, but True's flying career consisted of nothing but recklessly conducted training flights in which he was lucky to escape from the resultant crashes without killing himself.

The demand for pilots when True joined the R.F.C. was so urgent that he easily acquired his wings at Farnborough, but after he had crashed yet another plane at Gosport he was invalided out of the Flying Corps. This was in March 1916. Both his head and his hip were injured in the crash and it was the former hurt that was

blamed for his peculiar mental processes and his outbursts
of ill-tempered behaviour which then became more
frequent. But while he was in hospital the medical authorities learned about his drug-taking. When they gave him
morphia to relieve the pain of the hip injury it had no
result whatsoever, so inured was he to the effects of the
drug.

Despite True's appalling record as a flyer and the
medical details of his physical injuries and mental instability, as soon as he felt better he was able to obtain a job
as a test pilot for a Government aircraft factory. This was
at Yeovil where his activities became so peculiar that even
though there was such a shortage of flyers he was dismissed.

Thanks to his lavish monetary resources he could afford
to go to the United States, where he thoroughly enjoyed
himself, posing as a war pilot who had been injured in
combat with the enemy on the Western Front. The United
States had just entered the war and True was feted as a
thrilling guest who was able to recount the most remarkable air exploits. At one of the dinners that he attended
in New York he sat next to a pretty young actress named
Frances Roberts. She fell so deeply in love with this hero
from across the ocean that when he proposed marriage a
few days afterwards she immediately accepted him. Like
the girl in South Africa who married Heath, Miss Roberts
does not appear to have questioned her husband's stories
in any way, but she persuaded him that it was his patriotic
duty to help America to train pilots.

As a result he obtained a job at the United States Army
Flying School at Houston, Texas. Mrs. True remained in
New York to fulfil a theatrical engagement. She was quite
unaware that after a week or so at the flying school the
authorities had dismissed True as hopelessly incompetent.
He wandered around Mexico and Cuba before returning
to New York.

By that time the Armistice had been signed and the
couple came to England. There was still time for the
young wastrel to have mended his ways and to settle down

in a well-paid job which could have been arranged by his parents. Indeed there was every reason for True to look on the future with confidence. He had a devoted wife and she was soon to present him with a child. His mother was beside herself with joy to have her son back alive and more or less unharmed after a war which had taken so many young men.

But it was not to be. True became a worse wastrel than ever. His addiction to drugs was so serious that time after time he had to enter nursing homes for a cure, none of which did much good. Those who knew him really well regarded him as completely mad, particularly as he insisted that there was another man looking like him, behaving in the same way as he did, and actually named Ronald True.

When summonses came for unpaid bills, when bets went wrong, when there were rumours of affairs with other women, it was always this other mysterious person who was to blame.

Chance acquaintances, of whom Ronald True had scores (men seemed to be amused by him and many women were definitely mesmerised by his personality) did not seem to see anything incongruous in this absurd story of a double. True, who went around borrowing money off anyone he could, sometimes pilfering from the coats of fellow guests in houses that he visited, even stealing from shops and bookstalls just for the fun of it, was regarded as a delightful specimen of the Bright Young Things.

All this time his devoted wife and his long-suffering mother stood by him as best they could. Time after time they found him in Soho or some West End night club, dazed and morose after a drug debauch, and time after time they took him home until he ran away again. Then, early in 1922, they lost all trace of him.

Mrs. True became so alarmed that she went to Scotland Yard. At the time there was no evidence that her husband could be detained on suspicion of any crime and all that the police could do was to advise her to engage a private detective. This Mrs. True immediately did, but a few days later there was no need for the sleuth's services. Ronald True had been approached as he sat in a box at a Hammersmith music hall, and was arrested for murder.

And so in due course he stood in the dock at the Old Bailey before Mr. Justice McCardie.

His victim was a bright, twenty-five-year-old girl named Gertrude Yates. She was one of those butterflies who had left a steady job behind a shop counter when attracted by the glitter of the West End. Under the name of Olive Young she was well known in night clubs and the bars of the more popular hotels and restaurants.

Although at the time that True got to know her in some night club she had not actually drifted on the streets, she was in the habit of entertaining men friends in a small flat she had rented in Finborough Road, Fulham.

It was revealed during the trial of Heath that while the majority of women were greatly attracted to him there were one or two who seemed to sense that he was a dangerous man and they found him utterly repulsive. This exceptional feminine instinct about danger also applied in the case of Ronald True, and although in the months of 1921 after he had left his wife he had pursued a ceaseless round of amusement while making vain and glorious boasts of his flying enterprise and had infatuated many women, there were a few who were terrified of him. He roused a strong sense of dislike in Olive, despite the fact that she was an unprincipled little gold-digger, and True took good care to convince her that he was a man of means.

He persisted in worrying her despite rebuffs, calling at her house and continually telephoning her. On three nights in succession he ordered the chauffeur of the expensive limousine that he had hired to drive him to the corner of Finborough Road. On each of these occasions he either lost his courage at the last moment or found that Olive was out, for he soon returned to the car and was driven away. He made no secret of these visits and told friends various remarkable stories about a Fulham flat from which he intended to get money even if he had to commit murder.

Once again he drove to Finborough Road. It was 11 o'clock on a Sunday night and on this occasion Olive allowed him to enter. They spent the night together and shortly after dawn on the following morning True got up, saying that he intended to make some tea. When he returned from the kitchen with a tray bearing two cups, the drowsy girl did not see what he was concealing in his hand beneath the tray. It was a rolling pin.

True put the tray down and handed the cup of tea to Olive. She half sat up to drink it and from his position just behind her True brought the rolling pin down on her head. He gave her five crushing blows. She started to moan as she lay dying and to stifle the sound True grabbed a towel and thrust it so far into her open mouth that it completely jammed the gullet. Then just to make certain he took the girdle from her dressing gown and tied it round her neck. For some reason he dragged the corpse from the bed into the adjoining room which had been turned into a bathroom and left it sprawled on the floor.

He then took the pillows from his side of the bed and pushed them under the bedclothes to give the impression that a person was still sleeping there. Why he did this instead of simply pushing the corpse down in the bed and pulling the eiderdown over it is inexplicable.

One of the motives for his crime was that he was hard-pressed for ready cash. From his victim's handbag he obtained £8 in notes and silver, and from her dressing table a considerable amount of showy jewellery. He made no effort to leave the flat and was still there when the daily maid arrived at 9 o'clock—nearly two hours after the crime had been committed.

He muttered something to her about her mistress wanting to remain undisturbed until later in the morning and then bade the girl goodbye. Hardly had he entered the cruising taxi in the Fulham Road than the maid discovered the body and the hunt was on.

True drove to the West End where he visited an out-fitters and actually displayed to the assistant the blood-stains on his suit, saying that they were the result of a flying accident, for which reason he needed some new clothes right away. He then went to some of his old haunts, chatted amiably to a number of friends. To a particular crony he suggested that for their evening's entertainment they might dine together and then catch the second house at the Hammersmith Palace of Varieties where he understood there was a particularly good show.

Seldom can there have been a murder case of this type where Scotland Yard had such little trouble in identifying and tracking down the wanted man. Less than fourteen hours after he had brought that rolling pin crashing down on Olive Young's skull he was being questioned by the police.

This brief résumé of Ronald True's life and his crime —which leaves out scores of peculiarities which were later revealed—suggests incidentally that he must have been insane.

But in 1922 when he appeared in the Old Bailey dock this was by no means so obvious that the jury would almost automatically return a verdict of guilty but insane. There were doctors who thought True was mad and there were others who stated without reservations that he was not. Sir Richard Muir, who was Counsel for the Prosecution, was able to show that while the medical evidence offered by the defence on Ronald True's insanity was conclusive, it did not meet the requirements of the M'Naughton Rules.

For five days the legal battle swayed to and fro. The jury returned a verdict of guilty and True was sentenced to death.

His appeal was dismissed and thereupon the Home Secretary, who had examined the medical evidence of the trial, appointed a commission of three medical men to examine True and report on his state of mind. They were

unanimous in finding that Ronald True was a lunatic.
He was reprieved and sent to Broadmoor.

The uproar in the Press was such that at one time it was
seriously considered that it might bring down the Government. One reason was that only shortly before a young
man named Henry Jacoby, an hotel worker who had
murdered Lady White in circumstances of particular
brutality, had been hanged, despite a large public effort to
obtain a reprieve for him on account of his youth.

The failure to save young Jacoby from the scaffold was
now contrasted with the reprieve of True, regarded as a
foul monster who had brutally killed a so-called innocent
girl, who had managed to escape death on account of his
alleged aristocratic ancestry, the suggestion being that
powerful influences had been at work to persuade the
Home Secretary to save the murderer's life.

There was a stormy scene in the House of Commons at
question time when a flood of demands to know the reason
why the True scandal had arisen were made to the Home
Secretary. Calmly and cogently he gave the facts of the
Law and the House of Commons, at any rate, realised that
justice had indeed been done.

For myself, I had no doubt whatever that Ronald True
must have been irresponsible for his actions. I had seen,
as few except the warders who guarded him in the dock
had seen, what he had been doing during the major part
of that trial. His eyes were for the most time fixed on
something below the shelf of the dock. It is probable that
the public and the jury thought that he was making notes
or reading some piece of paper.

In actual fact he was playing with a small celluloid
duck, pushing it from one side to the other and trying to
produce swimming movements as it chased after non-
existent pieces of bread in the little duck pond which his
twisted brain had created so as to evade the boredom of
the trial.

If the appearances of Heath and True were those of
typical young Englishmen, the appalling ordinariness of

the sex murderer illustrates my point that there is no such thing as a murder characteristic in the face.

Imagine a little man in the late middle age, rather seedy and a little shabby—and you can see an example of him in any London street, in the buses and in the tubes. You feel rather sorry for him because obviously the battle of life has been too long and too vigorous and now, as he sees middle age fast approaching, he has obviously given up the fight to realise all those ambitions he had in youth. He may be a meek man, but he is usually a very honest person as well. Somewhere in the suburbs you imagine a plump little grey-haired wife who still has faith in him and who still loves him.

The particular example of this type of man of whom I am thinking was rather small, rather thin, and his dome-like head was almost bald. His eyes were bad and he wore a pair of National Health spectacles. He had not troubled to shave very closely, but his person was clean with a nice shirt and tie, and even though his suit was all too obviously ready-made and a bargain, it had been carefully pressed and brushed.

Through circumstances this man was jerked from the placid routine of his life which had ensured his anonymity for years. On the front pages of the newspapers his photograph had been published. Millions of readers were helping tens of thousands of police find him. He was a hunted man.

With very little money it was impossible to get out of the country or even to move to another town and put up at some discreet little hotel. All he could do was to stay a single night at some cheap lodging-house, to shuffle around the streets, to buy a cup of coffee and a ham roll at some coffee stall or transport café and occasionally to rest up in a derelict house on a bomb site.

Every street was crammed with people who knew what his face looked like, yet so ordinary was he, so typical of a thousand other men of his age and social position, that for days he was able to roam about London without being noticed. He walked past scores of evening newspaper posters on which the latest developments in the police hunt had been roughly scrawled by the newsvendors. He saw a policeman coming towards him and every nerve in his body grew tight as he wondered whether this time he would be stopped.

At last, when his money had all gone and he was hungry, dirty from sleeping out and his face was covered with a stubble of a three-days-old growth, he approached a passer-by in a street in Putney for the price of a cup of tea.

It was early in the morning and the suspicious circumstances influenced the stranger to tell the next policeman he met. The officer went in pursuit of the wanderer and discovered him standing wearily against the Embankment wall, gazing at the dirty water of the Thames. Without protest the man agreed to accompany the officer to the station, where he was given some bread and butter and a mug of hot tea. As he gratefully ate and drank the first refreshment he had had for many hours, he admitted that his name was George Reginald Halliday Christie. Very quietly he began to cry. . . .

When in due course he appeared in the dock at the Old Bailey his counsel, Mr. Curtis Bennett, submitted that Christie was as mad as a March hare. No one who had listened to the terrible story of his killings could have put up much argument to suggest that such a man was sane by the standards of a layman.

Undoubtedly the most terrible phase of this trial occurred during the three hours that Christie himself stood in the witness box, peering shortsightedly through his glasses at the Judge and jury, and giving his replies to counsel's questions in a soft, almost seductive voice, marred only by its incoherence.

I do not think I was alone among the people, who included notable writers and actors, when I say that my reaction was one of pitying wonder when Mr. Curtis Bennett asked him if Ruth Fuerst was his first victim.

He pondered for a moment, staring at the ceiling, as if trying to revive his memory.

Finally, with his wide-opened eyes enlarged by the lenses of his spectacles, he whispered: " I think so."

As Christie himself definitely appeared to be ignorant of the duration of his criminal exploits, and of the number of his victims, it will never be really known just how evil this man was, or how many women met their doom at his hands.

Sex perversion was the motive for most of his murders, but certainly not for all of them. Unbelievable as it may appear to be in the case of such a monster, his excuse for killing his wife was that he had been woken during the night because she was having convulsions. " I could not bear to see her suffer," he explained; " I got a silk stocking and put it round her neck and put her to sleep."

It is probable that this excuse of a fantastic form of pity for a woman to whom he had been married for nearly thirty years was not a true one. It was more likely that Mrs. Christie had come across some proof of her husband's murders and that she had hinted that she must go to the police. It was an undoubted fact that a week before he had killed her he had given up his job with British Road Services on the pretext that he had obtained a better one in Sheffield and he certainly forged an unposted letter that she had written to her sister so as to give the impression that she was still alive twenty-four hours after he had strangled her. Nevertheless, there was in this one murder none of the sex motive which presumably impelled him to commit the other crimes.

When Christie talked about his wife in Court he had to remove his spectacles and wipe the tears from his eyes while describing the happiness he had had with her and even more bizarre was the excuse he made for burying her body under the floor boards of his house. " I did not want to lose her," he said.

Mrs. Christie was killed on December 14, 1952. Christie had by that time committed three or four murders. The garden of his shabby little house in Rillington Place became a graveyard. The loss of his wife seems to have released the last lock on his terrible and perverted desires. Within two months of his wife's death he had committed three further murders.

Christie's first victim was believed to be Ruth Fuerst, aged twenty-one years when he murdered her in the summer of 1943. He was at the time a War Reserve policeman, and he got into conversation with the girl, an Austrian refugee, in a snack bar. When his wife went away for a short holiday with relatives in Sheffield he invited her to his home where he strangled her with a piece of rope. During the night he took her from the bedroom and put her under the floor boards in the kitchen. The body remained there for some time and it is probable that the smell became so bad that while his wife—who had returned from her holiday—was out at some evening entertainment, he buried the corpse in the garden during the blackout.

A few months later Christie was released from the police service on account of age, and it was then that he made the acquaintance of a new victim, Muriel Eady, who was thirty-two years of age. She worked in a radio factory at Park Royal. He first took her home in October 1944. On the third or fourth occasion she had a cold and he suggested that it might help if she inhaled some liquid which he had for the purpose of relieving catarrh. The woman agreed and Christie got a jar which had a metal lid. In this he inserted the flexible rubber tube from the gas pipe and then told Miss Eady to cover her head with a towel while she inhaled.

It is probable that the powerful aromatic smell of the inhalant banished any suspicion she might have had of the gas. She was, of course, soon unconscious and Christie then strangled her with a stocking. In due time her body was hidden in a small brick alcove in the yard which served as a wash house. By night he buried her in the garden of the house. Christie also claimed that he had killed

Mrs. Beryl Evans in November 1949. She was the wife of the tenant, Timothy Evans, and mother of a baby girl, who lived in the top floor flat. Both Mrs. Evans and her child were strangled and their bodies found by the police in the wash house, as a result of the husband walking into a police station at Merthyr Tydfil and confessing to both crimes.

Evans was charged at the Old Bailey on January 13, 1950, with the murder of his child and in due course hanged for it. As the result of Christie's claim that he had murdered Mrs. Evans there was considerable controversy after Christie's trial and the suggestion was made that there had been a miscarriage of justice in condemning Evans to death.

It must be remembered that Christie never claimed to have murdered the baby and that this was the crime for which Evans was hanged. What must be almost certain is that Christie assisted in the disposal of the bodies and it must have been a tremendous shock to him when Evans confessed to their murders, for presumably he would have in due course disposed of them in some way if only to lessen the chance of discovery of his own victims. Already his dog had dug up the skull of Ruth Fuerst.

After Mrs. Christie had been disposed of Christie's perversion was let loose in all its terrible force. He hungrily searched for more victims for his lust. What he did was to wander around the streets of the locality in which he lived and stop near the advertisement boards outside newsagent shops. When he saw a woman reading an announcement referring to the letting of a room he would get into conversation with her and mention that there was one available in his own house.

If the woman appeared to be interested he would then ask her a series of cleverly designed questions, so as to discover whether she had many relatives or friends in London. If he discovered that she was more or less on her own he would invite her to come round to see the room that he had available. Once he got her there he would start to talk about photography, a hobby in which he was genuinely interested, and suggest that he should take her photograph. There was a certain amount of vague evidence in some instances that the photographs he took of his women guests were obscene, but this was certainly not his normal habit.

The room in which he destroyed his victims was the kitchen. In the centre of the floor was a deck chair and in some way he always managed to get his visitor to sit down there. The house was an old one and still contained gas brackets which had, of course, been plugged when the electric mains were put in to provide illumination. One of these gas pipes Christie had unplugged and attached a length of flexible tubing to it. This tubing ran to the back of the deck chair and at some stage in the conversation he moved to the wall and turned on the tap. As soon as the woman started to become a little dizzy he moved across and strangled her.

What happened then is a topic which will interest psychiatrists and the medical profession for many generations to come. But after a nightmare interval and when some semblance of normality had returned to Christie he was faced with the problem of disposing of the body. The tiny garden could no longer be used. There were already mouldering corpses covered by a foot or so of soil and a few small stones to give the impression of a rockery.

In the adjoining living room his wife's body lay immediately below the floor boards. There were tenants upstairs. The only possible place of concealment was the kitchen itself. Confronted with the problem of getting rid of the body of Kathleen Maloney, whom he murdered during the first week of 1953, he trussed her naked and mutilated body up so that it would occupy the least possible space and jammed it in a coal cupboard beside the kitchen stove, nailing the wood and then pasting on wallpaper. A week later the corpse of Rita Nelson was pushed in beside Kathleen Maloney and finally a third victim, Hectorina MacLennan, was forced into the tiny hole as well.

THE MANIA OF MURDER

What suddenly impelled Christie to leave this house of death is not known. Possibly it may have been that there was literally no more room for the further victims he undoubtedly hoped to find, and secondly there was the growing curiosity of his wife's relatives as to what had happened to Mrs. Christie. It was inevitable once he had left the ground floor flat and strangers came in that the bodies of the three girls in the alcove and the already decomposing corpse of his wife under the living-room floor would be discovered.

Only the routine procedure of the police in starting to dig over the garden revealed that the man was a bigger murderer than even the terrible relics in the house indicated.

His trial before Mr. Justice Finnemore was naturally mainly concerned with the question of his sanity. The cold and impersonal medical evidence of the sexual perversion which motivated his crimes was so disgusting that no layman could hope to understand it. Psychiatric evidence that he was unaware of what he was doing was wrong at the time he committed the murders, was belied both by medical evidence taken while he was in prison and by the defendant's own almost horrifying calmness.

The Judge voiced the thoughts of all ordinary people in that Court when he said in his summing up: " The fact that a man acts like a monster, cruelly and wickedly, is not of itself evidence of his insanity." Christie was actually on trial only for the murder of his wife. The Judge told the jury it was probably a unique case in the history of crime, not only in this country, but perhaps in the whole world, for a defendant to announce calmly from the witness box, " Yes, I did kill her, and I killed six others as well." The nine men and three women of the jury discussed for almost one and a half hours whether Christie was a maniac or a cool and ultra-sane murderer who had found it convenient to boast of his mass killings in public so that normal decent people should consider that he must be mad.

The jury's verdict was that this was not the case of a maniac, and Christie was duly condemned to death. He heard his sentence with less emotion than he had shown when listening to the account of his wife's death, and he left the dock in the same calm and gentle manner in which he had conducted himself ever since he had been detained by that Putney policeman early one winter morning.

It is perhaps a justified plea for the retention of hanging that a man like Christie was better dead not only for the protection of the society which he menaced, but also for the peace of his own black and misguided soul.

Another story of the tragedy that can occur when the bonds of restriction which maintain human decency are burst asunder was the evidence produced during the trial in 1942 of Gordon Frederick Cummins, an airman of twenty-eight years of age.

He is believed to have been responsible for attacks, five of which were fatal, on eight women between October 1941 and February 1942. The war news was more important than this series of attacks and murders, but among the police of London, and certainly in the minds of very many women, the crimes were comparable with the infamous Jack the Ripper murders of 1888.

The first crime which, in its method, meant that Cummins must be suspected, concerned a nineteen-year-old girl named Mabel Church who was raped, robbed and strangled at Hampstead. Soon afterwards a forty-eight-year-old woman, Mrs. Edith Humphries, was robbed, and her skull and face battered in, in Gloucester Crescent, a quiet road close to Regents Park.

There was then an interval until the body of Miss Evelyn Hamilton, aged forty, was found by a passer-by in the narrow entrance to an air raid shelter at Montague Place, Marylebone, as soon as it was light in the morning of February 9, 1942. She had been gagged with her scarf and then strangled. Not far away her handbag was found empty.

This crime looked at first like a fairly routine case of

robbery with violence, where the attacker had probably gone farther than he intended and killed in an attempt to silence his victim, but the medical report showed more sinister motives behind the crime. The mass of bruises which covered her body had been caused by blows inflicted after death.

Within twenty-four hours a second murder was reported. This time the victim was Mrs. Evelyn Oatley, but who was known as Rita Ward, who was found in her flat at Wardour Street. Almost all her clothing had been ripped from her body which had been terribly slashed with a tin opener found in the room. Once again there was an empty handbag nearby. Three nights after that a third murder was discovered. The victim, a woman known under the names of Margaret Lowe and Peggy Campbell, was found terribly mutilated in her flat in a small street off Tottenham Court Road. The weapon used for the mutilation of the body on this occasion was a potato peeler.

Within a matter of minutes of Scotland Yard detectives going to investigate this crime, a fourth was reported which must have been committed within a matter of an hour or two of the murder of Florence Lowe. The latest victim was Mrs. Doris Jouannet. Mrs. Jouannet was lying on a bed strangled in the same way as the others. The maltreatment of her body had been carried out with a razor.

Even detectives hardened by experience to the activities of sex maniacs were shocked at the extent of the injuries perpetrated on these unfortunate women. Yet there is a pattern even in sexual mania, and that pattern was absent in these cases. The injuries were spectacular rather than symbolic of some perverted activity. With medical opinion to support this theory, the police became more interested in the empty handbags and ransacked rooms. It was obvious that the murders had been committed for the sake of the few pounds and coins in the women's handbags, and the mutilations had been deliberately and cold-bloodedly produced in order to suggest that a sex maniac had been at work. But the killer had been careless. Fingerprints were found on both the can opener and the potato peeler —and they matched. By the time Mrs. Jouannet met her doom he had taken the precaution of wearing gloves and no prints were discovered.

Whoever the killer was, he had roamed London so as to spread his activities. At the outset the strained police forces worked separately at divisional level, and each of the four deaths had occurred in a different division. But in time, as the reports were collated at Scotland Yard, the overall picture of a mass murderer at large who was perfectly ready to kill at intervals of a few hours emerged. Simultaneously routine reports of minor offences added to the picture. On the evening prior to the murders of Mrs. Lowe and Mrs. Jouannet two women had been assaulted. One, walking through the blackout in the Paddington area, had not suffered greatly, but the other, Mrs. Greta Heywood, attacked in a shop doorway near Jermyn Street, had been almost strangled. Only the arrival of a passer-by who peered through the darkness saved her from death. Her assailant ran off and she went to Bow Street police station to report the attack.

A constable returned with her to the scene of the assault and there found a service respirator case. Inside the flap the R.A.F. service number of its owner had been stamped. It was a matter of an hour to check with the Air Ministry the airman's name and whereabouts.

So suspicion turned on Gordon Cummins, stationed in a block of flats near the Zoo which had been commandeered by the R.A.F. for air crews under training. The respirator was examined and in the compartments made for goggles and first-aid kit a few trinkets were discovered. Their ownership was traced to four of the dead women. After Cummins had been detained and taken to Brixton Prison on remand his fingerprints were taken. They matched those on the mutilation weapons.

At his trial his callous attitude as he listened to the horrific story of his crimes was repellent. Equally unpleasant was his sneering contempt for everyone—his counsel, the Judge, and the relatives of his victims. He protested his innocence to the end.

His motive had, as the police suspected, been simply to get money. An airman's pay was insufficient for his expensive tastes. He pretended to his comrades that he was actually the Honourable Gordon Cummins, and the scion of an aristocratic family. He used to give parties simply to impress Dominion volunteers for air crew—some of whose wallets he had pilfered in order to entertain them—before he hit on the diabolical idea of creating a picture of sex maniac in order to disguise his crude requirements of cash for black market whisky and the hire of a few tawdry girls to amuse his guests.

CHAPTER NINE

People with Guns

WHENEVER IN RECENT YEARS THERE HAS
been a trial at the Old Bailey of a gunman people have
said to me, "What a change there has been in things
since the war. The gangster is a symptom of the terrible
times we live in."

There have indeed in recent years been outrageous
crimes by unprincipled and utterly amoral rogues who
are ready to shoot to kill at the slightest provocation. This
is the inevitable aftermath of war, but I would stress that
things are certainly little worse than in the years gone by.

One of the first major trials I attended right at the
outset of my career was concerned with a vicious shooting
affray in a London street. The prisoners were two—a man
and a woman. They provided a remarkable contrast in
character, although it would be difficult to say which was
the more reprehensible.

The woman was charged under the name of May
Vivienne Churchill, but she was better known to the police
of two continents and to the newspaper readers of the
world as Chicago May. Few women who have stood in the
Old Bailey dock have had a better claim to beauty. Even
though she was by then approaching middle age, Chicago
May had the figure of a Gaiety Girl, red hair that Titian
would have painted with enthusiasm and a smile that was
designed to captivate her worst enemy—and frequently
did.

The prisoner who stood beside her was a sulky and
rather undersized young man who was obviously terrified
of the possible fate that awaited him. He was Charles
Smith, Chicago May's current lover.

The charge was shooting with intent to kill Eddie

Guerin, who was possibly the most famous professional criminal of the time because he was one of the very few men who had ever succeeded in escaping from the French penal colony of Devil's Island and lived to tell the tale.

The crime for which Guerin had been sent there was the real origin of the shooting which brought May and Smith to the Old Bailey dock, although the reason why it should have done so was never made clear in the evidence.

May was born in Ireland. She emigrated to the United States in the 'nineties and was for a time a chorus girl in *The Belle of New York*. She made a rich but unfortunate marriage, became a dope addict, and lost her stage job. Soon she was living in Chicago with Eddie Guerin, a thief and trickster with a long record of imprisonments in both Europe and America.

When the United States became too hot for them they came to Britain where both indulged in blackmail and robbery in order to obtain the capital for a major coup which had long interested Guerin. This was to rob the safe of the American Express Company in Paris. It was known that very large sums in many currencies and in gold were kept there for the firm's wealthy tourist clients.

The robbery was carried out without trouble, but someone in the underworld of Paris evidently " narked " and both May and Guerin were arrested. Guerin was sentenced to life imprisonment but May, using that innocent smile on the responsive French, was regarded as just a dupe and got off with a three-year sentence.

As soon as she was out of prison she came to London where she launched the biggest blackmail campaign the Metropolitan Police have ever had to tackle. With a corps of " husbands " to burst in at the appropriate moment to exert the necessary pressure to extract money, she set about captivating every man of rank and wealth she could entice with her charm and chatter.

How many men were bled white by this gang will never be known, for the police were discreet about the letters they found in May's Northumberland Avenue flat from men in high public office, well known in legal circles, and in the Peerage.

Smith was probably one of May's blackmail operators as well as her lover when Guerin reached England and inferred that he felt entitled to share the proceeds of May's exploits. She did not agree and took steps to silence her one-time lover for good.

She knew that Guerin was living with a woman in the Bloomsbury district. Late one June night in 1907 she was sitting with Smith in a cab that slowly meandered around the streets of that area. Then, in Russell Square, she saw Guerin strolling along the pavement towards the tube station.

At May's cry of triumph Smith leaped from the cab and fired six shots at Guerin, who hobbled to cover, hit in the foot.

A constable immediately gave chase and Smith aimed the revolver at him, pulling the trigger on a fortunately empty chamber. Both May and he were in custody within a couple of minutes of the attack.

The only possible defence was that Smith had no intention of killing but wished merely to scare Guerin. Despite the fact that his aim had been so bad the plea was not proven. Nor was there any sympathy for Chicago May who tried to show that she had learned Guerin intended to burn her face with vitriol unless she returned to him.

The famous Mr. Justice Darling was the judge, and he imposed a sentence of fifteen years on May, who smiled and bowed to the Court as if she was making her exit from the stage after prolonged applause.

Smith was sentenced to penal servitude for life. It took him a full minute to understand, and then he began to gibber and foam at the mouth, a stream of obscenities and curses on the Judge pouring from his lips. He struggled and bit the warders who closed in on him and he had to be carried bodily down the stairs. He was typical of the gunman of any age: they are all gutless when the inevitable punishment for their wrongdoing is administered.

Chicago May was sent back to the United States just after the end of the First World War, and Smith, who was also an American, was deported in 1922.

Smith's struggle with the warders in the dock was a mild affair compared with the trouble caused by a couple of prisoners who, I think, were the toughest renegades I have ever seen. Thirty years have passed since I watched Browne and Kennedy in the dock, but the vicious brutality of their characters remains as vivid as if it was only yesterday.

Frederick Guy Browne and William Kennedy were gunmen. Browne was possibly the worse of the two. At the age of twenty-seven, in 1910, he had first fallen foul of the law for carrying firearms. The moment he was out of prison he went in for armed robbery, arson, burglary and assaults. So strong was his belief that brute force was the only thing that mattered that he followed a rigorous course of physical culture. He did not drink and he did not smoke. In and out of prison, he finally received a stiff sentence in 1923 which he served at Parkhurst. There he simply refused to work, attacked the warders and lost all remission marks as well as being put in solitary confinement for periods of varying length. He was released in April 1927.

Kennedy was a prison crony, known as " Two-gun Pat "; he boasted about being a Sinn Feiner who had killed several soldiers. The two met while at Dartmoor where Kennedy was serving a sentence for robbery. Although he was a desperate and violent man he had neither the brains nor the courage of Browne, and he could, I suppose, be described as the dupe of the stronger charactered man.

After Browne came out of prison he rented the Globe Garage in Northcote Road, Clapham Junction, where he employed Kennedy as a clerk, the main activities being concerned with the gang of office thieves and burglars which Browne was organising.

But ostensibly the garage was a perfectly normal place. There were efficient mechanics there, and Browne himself had a good engineering knowledge. People round about regarded him as a hot-tempered but reliable man, and in the row of neat little houses in nearby Sisters Avenue where he lived with his wife and little daughter neighbours considered him an ideal husband and father. Strangely enough, he was everything they believed so far as his domestic life was concerned.

Not one vestige of his criminal activities was ever allowed to contaminate that home. He lavished money on its furnishings and on his family—but without ostentation or undue luxury. His great ambition was to arrange for his daughter to go to the finest school the country could provide, and with money for the fees a minor problem he directed all his energies to seeing that she was well spoken and beautifully mannered. His wife was a charming woman, utterly devoted to her husband. She obviously knew about his prison record but she regarded his " business career " as a thing apart from his domestic life.

In fairness this decent side of Browne needs to be recorded, for it is all that can be said in his favour. The London and provincial police regarded him as one of the worst crooks ever to pass through their hands and the moment notification came from the Home Office that he was once again out of prison there were many realistic officers who accepted that someone would probably get hurt arresting him for his next offence.

But the crime he and his fellow-crook committed was so brutal that horror for a time banished these thoughts.

An early worker travelling along an Essex country lane between Ongar and Romford saw a rivulet of congealed blood on the road, leading to a grassy bank. There he saw a policeman lying dead, his helmet beside him, his notebook a few feet away and a pencil in his right hand.

His head was a bloody mess of torn flesh, and both eyes had been shot out. The constable was P.C. Gutteridge, a married man with years of reliable service. He was found at six in the morning of September 26, 1927. He had last been seen by a fellow constable on the adjoining beat at 3.30 a.m. about five hundred yards from the place where he had been murdered.

Detectives were soon on the scene. A doctor reported that five of the shots, most of which would have caused instantaneous death, had been followed by two shots through the constable's eyes after he was dead. Detectives were satisfied that there had been no struggle, and the fact that Gutteridge had withdrawn his notebook and pencil while his torch remained in his pocket suggested that he was about to make notes in the headlights of a vehicle when he was attacked without warning. Some faint tyre marks just off the road indicated that a car had indeed stopped there.

Scotland Yard was immediately called in and the hunt for the killer was put in the hands of Chief Inspector James Berrett. He concentrated on finding the car, and he had a shrewd idea of the one he was looking for. Three hours after the body of the policeman had been discovered a doctor at Billericay reported to the local police that in the early hours of the morning his Morris Cowley car had been stolen from his garage. He had left his cases of surgical dressings and instruments in the car when he had locked it away the previous evening.

At almost the same time as this report a constable in Brixton had noticed a car standing in Foxley Road. Enquiries showed that it did not belong to any of the people living nearby, and it was treated as an abandoned and possibly stolen vehicle. By mid-morning the Essex police report of the doctor's stolen car was matched with the Brixton discovery, and detectives proceeded to examine the vehicle with minute care.

A mudguard had been scratched and dented, and there were splashes of blood on the running board. Under the near-side front seat a used revolver cartridge was found.

Ballistic experts said that the bullets embedded in the

skull of the dead man were of a very old type, and that
the cartridge case in the car had been made prior to 1894.

It was fortunate that the doctor who owned the car kept
a very careful schedule of his mileage, and he had jotted
down the speedometer figure on the previous evening.
The instrument now recorded an additional forty-two
miles, which was almost exactly the distance from Billericay to Brixton via Romford and Ongar on the route where
Gutteridge had been killed.

Hundreds of criminals who were known to carry arms
were rounded up and questioned. Browne, who naturally
came under suspicion, was the subject of special enquiries.
The ostensible honesty of his garage and the placidity of
his home life, plus no evidence whatever that he had been
out on the fatal night, forced the police to hold their hand
until they could get more facts.

It was not until January that Browne's own criminal
activities brought him into the police net. A car was stolen
from Tooting and the description of the man seen in it
tallied closely with that of Browne. The car was traced
to Sheffield where the thief had exchanged it for a sports
car. In this he had driven to Dartmoor to pick up an
ex-convict due for release. After dropping his friend on
the outskirts of London he continued to the Brixton
garage where a dozen armed police were waiting.

They were on the driver before he could do anything
—which was just as well, for he had a loaded revolver
clipped to the door of the car and another behind the
driver's seat. The man was, of course, Browne. In the
garage was a veritable armoury—and several of the medical
instruments which the doctor had left in the Morris
Cowley.

Browne remained defiant, certain that the police could
never prove that he had been in Essex on that September
night, but his vicious temper resulted in him showing that
murder was certainly not repellent to him.

"If you had stopped me in the car on the road I would
have shot the five of you," he said to a detective, "and

saved one for myself. What I can see of it, I shall have to get a machine gun for you bastards next time."

Kennedy was away when the police arrested Browne. He had got married and gone off on his honeymoon. Returning to the garage a day or two later, the sight of the closed doors and two plain clothes men loitering outside gave him sufficient warning to flee to Liverpool with the idea of getting out of the country.

In Liverpool an officer, Detective Sergeant Mattinson, recognised Kennedy from the photographs in the *Police Gazette* and went up behind him. Kennedy whipped round and drew a gun, thrusting it against the Sergeant's heart. But he had forgotten to release the safety catch and the click of the hammer was not followed by the searing explosion this courageous officer had expected. He grabbed the barrel of the revolver and wrenched it downwards. After a bitter struggle Kennedy was pinioned and taken to the station to be charged.

Kennedy was taken to London and questioned. He insisted that he had not murdered P.C. Gutteridge but admitted that he knew who had. He made a long and carefully thought out statement which told the truth wherever there was corroborative evidence but put the blame for the actual shooting entirely on Browne. As regards the shooting of both eyes, Browne had done this because of his belief that the pupils of a murdered person photographed the scene at the moment of death for all time. "What are you looking at me like that for?" he was supposed to have shouted at the dead man.

And so these two outlaws in due time appeared at the Old Bailey jointly charged with murder. The Judge was Mr. Justice Avory. Kennedy wisely decided not to give evidence, preferring no doubt not to be questioned on his statement that he had been there but had been an unwilling witness of murder.

Browne, still vain and contemptuous, was only too eager to talk to the jury. He seemed almost amused about his confederate's statement. He insisted that he had been sleeping at home with his wife on the night of the murder and that if the Court had any sense it would order the police to find the boozing companion of Kennedy's who had put him up to fixing him with an alibi by blaming Browne.

Gradually his confidence disappeared, and the extraordinary number of warders on duty grew taut as they awaited the almost inevitable rumpus when the prisoners heard the jury's verdict and tried to retaliate like the trapped animals they were.

It came quite suddenly, with Browne fighting like a madman. Kennedy was more half-hearted for he was, I think, basically a coward. As suddenly the trouble was over, and the reaction was complete. Both men, perhaps in the hopes of some last-minute miracle of mercy and perhaps because even their twisted, brutish minds had been impressed, admitted that they had had a fair trial before they were led away.

The woman with the gun is, of course, a rarity. Even in American crime films the gangster's moll seems to have no part to play beyond looking pretty and aiding and abetting. She does not shoot her way out herself.

There are many records of women who have used firearms in unpremeditated murder, but I can recall only one notable trial where a woman deliberately went out seeking her victims with a gun—and she was eventually adjudged insane.

The trial was not well known because it occurred at the height of the invasion scare in 1940, and bizarre as the details were there was more important news for the tiny newspapers of the time.

The story begins some time before war broke out when a married couple, Mr. and Mrs. Fisher, who lived at Twickenham, fell out. They went their own ways, and each began living with a lover. Mrs. Fisher's companion, a foreigner, is of no importance to the case, and indeed was hardly mentioned at the trial. Mr. Fisher fell in love with a young widow, Florence Iris Ouida Ransom. She was quite well off and owned a farm in Oxfordshire.

Perhaps for reasons of discretion Fisher did not spend much time there. He took a cottage at Matfield, near Tonbridge, Kent, and there Mrs. Ransom was in the habit of staying at weekends.

Possibly through the dangers of invasion and bombs the couple abandoned this practice early in 1940 and Mr. Fisher went openly to live at his mistress' farm. Mrs. Fisher, with a daughter aged nineteen, became the tenant of the Kent cottage, the arrangement evidently being a perfectly friendly one, for since the couple had sorted out their matrimonial troubles to their own satisfaction they had been on good terms with one another. In fact, as soon as the blitz started Mr. Fisher often travelled down to the cottage to assure himself that all was well. He also provided money so that a housekeeper could be engaged.

These visits apparently aroused the jealousy of Mrs. Ransom. On July 8 she borrowed a gun from her brother, ostensibly to shoot rabbits, and took the train to London.

No one knows exactly what her movements were from the time she got on the train at Aylesbury until she arrived back at the farm late the same night, except that a railway porter made a rather unsatisfactory identification of her leaving Tonbridge Station from which a bus could be taken to Matfield, and a taxi driver thought he saw her taking the London train late in the afternoon.

But during that day death struck the cottage. Shots in that area, crammed with troops manning the first defence lines and training continually, went quite unnoticed, and the time of the attack remains unknown beyond the vague estimate obtainable from examination of the corpses later on.

While preparing tea for four people Mrs. Fisher and her daughter had been shot in the back and the housekeeper had half her skull blown off while standing or fleeing through an adjacent coppice. The house was in terrific disorder, but nothing of value was missing.

How the assailant, clearly on friendly terms as the evidence of the tea things indicated, had contrived to load and re-load several times, still managing to kill the victims by shots from the rear, is a mystery. There must have been many seconds between each shot, and the housekeeper, who had been attacked last and at very close range, would have had minutes in which to escape.

The most valuable clue left in the cottage of death was a woman's white leather glove. It was proved to be the property of Mrs. Ransom.

Her defence at her Old Bailey trial in November 1940 was that for the whole of the day of the crime her mind had been a complete blank. This so familiar excuse when evidence is damning was, I think, on this occasion probably true.

Mrs. Ransom had a record of mental instability and had been a voluntary patient on a number of occasions. Her appearance in the dock confirmed this view. She was a physically beautiful woman with red hair, healthy-looking, but with a strange brooding look in her eyes that betokened madness. Nevertheless she endured hours of cross-examination without turning a hair.

Mr. Justice Tucker, in the absence of medical evidence proving her insanity, had to sentence her to death, but she was soon afterwards pronounced insane and was sent to Broadmoor.

The gun killers who received their just deserts at the Old Bailey after the Second World War alarmed and horrified all law-abiding people because in the main they were very young. One of the worst of these cases concerned the shooting down in the street of Alec d'Antiquis on April 29, 1947.

The tragedy occurred soon after the attempted robbery of a pawnbrokers in Charlotte Street, Soho. Three masked men were involved, two attacking the assistants and a third firing indiscriminately from the doorway.

The staff, which included a man of seventy, showed great courage, and the crooks became frightened and ran to their car. The road was blocked with traffic so they abandoned the car and began running towards Tottenham Court Road. D'Antiquis, on a motor cycle, turned across their path and he was immediately shot down. Although many people hurried to the scene the three men got away. The shot man, who had a wife and six children, died before he reached hospital.

The police had a good description of the men, and soon valuable clues were forthcoming. In a block of offices in Tottenham Court Road a car key, a raincoat, cap and gloves were found.

The key belonged to the car used in the hold-up which had been stolen from a nearby street. The raincoat came from a firm of multiple tailors, and they could show from their records that it was part of a delivery to three of their London branches. Eventually the manager of the Deptford branch identified the coat, and he was able to show that it had been sold five months before to a Mr. Thomas, of Park Buildings, Peckham.

The name Thomas did not tally with the occupants of the house, Mr. and Mrs. Kemp. The woman's attitude—she admitted the existence of the coat but said it had been stolen from a public house long before—did not satisfy the police. They saw to it that Kemp was questioned before he could talk to his wife, and his story was that he had lost the coat at a cinema. Finally the wife said she had lent it to her brother, Charles Jenkins.

Jenkins was found and questioned. Confronted with the coat, he became alarmed and refused to say more, but later he claimed that it had been lent to Bill Walsh, who, Jenkins said, was somewhere in Southend. This was the traditional lack of honour among thieves, for the police knew Walsh and Jenkins had committed crimes together.

But Jenkins was at least speaking the truth as regards Walsh's whereabouts. The Southend police found some watches stolen during a night robbery in Bayswater and a gun which had been used in that crime. But Walsh had gone into hiding.

While the search for Walsh went on the police rounded up and questioned Terence Rolt, a boy of seventeen, and a young man named Geraghty, wanted for the Bayswater crime. Both denied that they had anything to do with the Charlotte Street hold-up, and they were released.

Then Walsh was found. He admitted his participation in the Bayswater robbery and went on to say that he had looked around Charlotte Street in company with Jenkins and Geraghty but he denied any part in the actual crime.

Confronted with this information Geraghty became more talkative and as a result young Rolt was again brought in for questioning. He broke down, saying that his bungling of the plan had caused the trouble, and gave damning details of what had happened.

Jenkins, Geraghty and Rolt were charged with murder. Their trial began on July 21, 1947, before Mr. Justice Hallett. Jenkins, the man who had actually worn the raincoat, was a cocky vicious renegade whose vanity was such that he believed he could lie his way out. He brought along a motley crowd of witnesses in the best tradition of a cheap Hollywood thriller, to provide him with an alibi. He was a rat who had not hesitated to try to involve a fellow-crook in order to save his own skin, and he showed not the slightest interest in the fate of the other two prisoners.

These—Rolt and Geraghty—relied on evidence that while they had set out to rob they had no intention of killing anyone. But Rolt had stolen guns from a warehouse, and it was Geraghty's gun which killed d'Antiquis.

It took the jury forty-five minutes to find all three guilty. Jenkins, a brute who had attacked two policemen in his 'teens, and Geraghty, one of the worst inmates that even Borstal institutions had ever known, were sentenced to death. Rolt was too young to be hanged, and he was ordered to be detained during His Majesty's pleasure.

It was only after the trial that I learned that Jenkins was a member of an infamous family. Two years before Thomas Jenkins, the elder brother, had been convicted for the manslaughter of Captain Robert Binney who had tried to intercept a car on London Bridge which Jenkins and his fellow-gangsters were using to get away from a smash-and-grab raid in the City. Jenkins was sentenced to eight years' imprisonment for this crime, and as soon as he was out—in 1952—he reverted to crime.

Once more I was to see a member of the Jenkins family in the Old Bailey dock. In March 1953 Thomas Jenkins stood there with two other hardened criminals—very lucky not to be facing a murder charge.

A month previously they had attempted an armed hold-up of a clerk bringing money for the wages of employees at a Hackney factory. The police had learned of the possibility and the factory staff were acting under instructions with police poised for action in the vicinity.

The men got away, pursued by the police. One, Robert Sandes, fired at a constable who pluckily closed with him, although wounded in the face and numbed by a bullet which tore through his raincoat belt. Jenkins also resisted like a madman, but did not use his gun. He was sent to prison for five years and Sandes for life.

Two brothers are also the leading figures in the story of men with guns in the post-war period.

The trial of Craig Senior and Burney in the autumn of 1952 was a routine affair. The police learned that they were in possession of stolen furs and clothing, and they planned to raid their house in Kensington.

Burney was awake and ran out of the house, being over-powered as he tried to climb a wall. Craig was asleep in a locked room. A woman opened the door and as the police rushed in Craig was seen to thrust his hand under the pillow. Two policemen grabbed his arm before he could withdraw the gun and fire. The safety catch was off and all chambers loaded. Both men were found guilty at the Old Bailey of robbery while armed and robbery with violence. Craig was also convicted of possessing a firearm with intent to endanger life. Both men received long sentences.

THE GUILTY AND THE INNOCENT

A week or so later this trial was recalled as the origin of the most tragic and horrible gun crime of recent years. Late on a dull November night—a Sunday—Croydon police were told of interlopers in a warehouse. Half a dozen police went to the scene and learned that the suspects were on the roof.

Detective-constable Fairfax climbed a drainpipe and saw two figures crouching near a chimney stack. He identified himself as a police officer and ordered them to come out.

A boyish voice replied: "If you want us—come and get us."

Fairfax did so. He grabbed one figure, who struggled free, shouting "Let him have it, Chris!"

A gun roared and the officer spun round with a bullet in his shoulder. He got hold of the man he had grabbed first and pulled him behind a low wall as another shot rang out.

Another policeman, P.C. McDonald, was now at the top of the pipe. Fairfax helped him over the coping as a third shot was fired. A third officer appeared, and as soon as he was silhouetted against the sky, the gunman fired at him as well.

More police were on the way. They had got into the warehouse and used the interior staircase to reach the roof. The leading officer, P.C. Miles, was shot between the eyes as he emerged on the roof. The assailant immediately fired again at the second officer, P.C. Harrison, shouting at the same time: "I'm Craig. You've given my brother twelve years. Come on, coppers. I'm only sixteen."

The second young rogue, whose name was Bentley, then bawled out: "Look out, Chris; they're taking me." This was the cue for yet another shot from Craig.

Soon afterwards armed police arrived and Craig, pulling the trigger on empty chambers, leaped over the side of the building, almost into a policeman's arms twenty-five feet below. The boy was badly hurt, but still screamed a defiant challenge: "I hope I've killed the —— lot."

Both Craig and Bentley were charged with murder.

Bentley was a typically unprincipled and feckless young man, and his weak intellect—more than made up by animal cunning—was evident from his behaviour in the dock.

Craig was as tragic a human being as I have ever seen in the dock, although I could feel no pity for him. My sorrow was for the widow of his victim and his parents. He and his thug of a brother came from a good home. Their father was a bank official, and the house in a pleasant residential suburb of Croydon had provided every comfort and privilege of the middle class.

Why should these two boys, educated and reared in a law-abiding environment among people who felt ashamed if they fell foul of the law even for a minor misdemeanour like exceeding the speed limit, have turned out the social outlaws that they were?

Other boys read horror comics ; other boys played at gangsters ; other boys loved crime films—and came to no harm.

The tragedy of that sullen and secretly frightened boy standing in the dock while the Judge sentenced his moronic comrade to death and Craig himself to be detained during Her Majesty's pleasure was the failure of society to make him a decent citizen despite all the favourable chances that had surrounded him.

CHAPTER TEN

Some Strange Cases

A PECULIAR MURDER CASE, WITH THE MOST unusual motive I have ever heard, was that of San Dwee, a Burmese elephant keeper employed at the London Zoo. He was tried in November 1928, before Mr. Justice Swift, for the murder of Sayed Ali.

San Dwee was obviously both bewildered and terrified by the ritual of British judicial procedure, and he must have felt even more bereft of a friend when the defence called no evidence on his behalf, on the submission that there was no case to go to the jury in the material put forward by the prosecution.

His woeful little brown face, with the dark eyes darting hither and thither, showed no relief even when the Judge, displaying the fairness of the Court, severely trounced the authorities for keeping him at the police station for thirty-six hours before charging him with murder.

Doubtless the prisoner realised that his pathetic lying had availed nothing and that these all-wise white men knew that he had committed what was indeed a callous and unnecessary murder.

He knew very little English and the details of the crime had to be pieced together from the few facts that he was able to give and from the background of the man's life.

Londoners may recall that after the second year of the Empire Exhibition of Wembley in 1925 the Zoo was fortunate enough to obtain a sacred white elephant. It arrived under the charge of San Dwee, but the English climate did not suit this very valuable animal and it was soon returned to its native land.

If San Dwee had gone back also with it all would have been well. He elected to stay in view of the pleasant working conditions at the Zoo, but soon pined for his

154

beloved elephant, for not only had it been a great honour to be chosen as its keeper but as is invariable he had expected to remain as its sole human companion until one or other of them died.

But there was one compensation. The head elephant keeper, the Indian Sayed Ali, was always permitted to return to his home in Calcutta during the winter months. While he was away San Dwee was acting head keeper, which was not merely an honour but a very profitable job as well, for he rode the elephant that gave children rides, and the stream of pennies handed to the animal and passed to its mahout with the trunk became San Dwee's property. When Sayed Ali returned, the Burmese lost both the prestige of the job and the extra income that went with it.

The two men slept in the same building in the Zoo, and one night, without so far as is known any preliminary quarrel, San Dwee grabbed a sledgehammer and battered Sayed Ali to death. Next he broke open a large wooden box in which the Indian kept his private possessions. There were his savings, a Post Office bank book, and a pile of coppers.

Having broken open the box San Dwee's courage failed him, and he did not take the money.

Next he injured himself in the foot with a pickaxe, climbed out of the window, and lay down behind a hedge where his groans attracted the attention of a police constable on duty in the Outer Circle of Regent's Park.

The officer climbed over the railings and in the light of his torch discovered the wounded man, who was moaning and gibbering in a mixture of Burmese and English. His story was that burglars had broken into the building where he lived with Sayed Ali, attacked the head keeper, and then went for him, but he had escaped. None of the clues at the scene of the crime supported the story.

The poor little man's interminable references to his beloved white elephant and his longing for his own country indicated the motive for the crime. He did not seem to realise that one word from him to the Zoo authorities

THE GUILTY AND THE INNOCENT

would have instantly produced a paid passage, while his own savings were quite sufficient for him to establish himself in comfort in Burma until he obtained a job.

He was sentenced to death but the sentence was quickly commuted, and four years later the Home Office accepted the recommendation of a Board that he be released and returned to his native land.

His was a futile crime, a brutal one, and his victim had done nothing to arouse his hate. Yet I think that most people in the Court felt pity for the tiny little Burmese whose only passion in life was elephants and who did not seem to understand—despite the gentleness of his Buddhist religion—that "thou shalt not kill" is a universal commandment applying to both East and West.

To be tried twice for murder at the Old Bailey— acquitted once and condemned once—was the unique record of Frederick Herbert Field, whose two trials were undoubtedly the most remarkable on a capital charge. The strangeness was enhanced by the fact that no one had the slightest personal doubts that he was guilty of the first crime despite the legal necessity of returning a verdict of "Not Guilty", and then the second trial created tremendous legal interest because there seemed to be a distinct possibility that the prisoner's cunning might give him his freedom a second time.

Field was in the classic tradition of born killers in that he was blessed—or cursed—with considerable charm, was good-looking, vain and intelligent. The factual record of his private life suggested that he was happily married, with a good wife and pretty little daughter.

But beneath this very normal exterior were secret emotional currents which branded him as a degenerate. One or two details of his activities immediately prior to his murders which were hinted at in Court and were divulged to me by police officers who had access to the dossiers on the crime indicated that Field was the slave of monstrous lusts.

The first crime for which he entered the Old Bailey

dock occurred in September 1931 when a young prostitute who was known in Soho as Norma Laverick but was in fact Nora Upchurch was found strangled. She haunted the streets of Soho and took her clients to her room in Pimlico. Well known to the police, she disappeared from the streets towards the end of September.

On the morning of October 2 two decorators who had the keys of an empty shop in Shaftesbury Avenue went to the premises to tidy up and do some painting. One of them was Frederick Field. His superior led the way into the murky interior and, seeing a figure lying on the ground, stubbed it with his umbrella, saying " We'll have to shift these old wax models."

It was no wax model, but the corpse of Nora Upchurch. She had been strangled, and in the opinion of Sir Bernard Spilsbury had been dead for about three days.

At the inquest profound suspicions fell on Field because it was shown that he had possession of a key to the shop and he was unable to give a completely satisfactory explanation of what had happened to it. Nevertheless, when a verdict of " murder against a person or persons unknown " was returned no move was made to arrest Field.

The world trade depression was on, Field lost his job, and joined the Royal Air Force. Months went by, and then Field, on pass from his camp, walked into the editorial offices of a national newspaper and demanded to see the news editor. A reporter was sent to interview him, and Field handed over a neatly written confession of the murder of Nora Upchurch. The editor already knew of Field for at the time of the inquest there had been a tentative arrangement for the newspaper to pay for his defence if he should be charged with murder. The briefest perusal of the detailed confession indicated that this was no crank's vapourings but an authentic description of a terrible crime.

Scotland Yard was informed, and Field was taken away for questioning. After the usual warning, he was cross-examined and gave details every bit as descriptive as those in the written confession. But he was extremely clever over a number of points. For example, he said that he had throttled the girl to death with his bare hands, while the mark of some material on the skin of the neck proved beyond all doubt that a belt or cord had been used. He was also insistent that he had never met Norah Upchurch before the night he killed her, whereas many witnesses could testify that the girl had gone around in fear of her life for weeks before she was killed.

In due course he was committed for trial at the Old Bailey. When the date was set he withdrew his confession, saying that he had made it simply to get money from the newspaper.

In court the prosecution was faced with the impossible task of proving a case on which there was no evidence against Field beyond that of his own confession. Mr. Justice Swift had no recourse except to stop the case and direct the jury to return a verdict of Not Guilty. Field, with a very smug expression walked out of the dock to freedom. His new attitude to the faked confession was that he had been compelled to make it so that the cloud of suspicion over him could be dispelled.

Three years passed—and once again that erect and lithe young figure, in immaculate R.A.F. uniform, stood in the dock on a charge of murder. He undoubtedly thought he had hit upon a scheme of murdering without risk of punishment, for his second crime was uncannily similar to the first in every detail but one—the final scenes of the trial.

Field's second victim was Beatrice Sutton, a prostitute living at Clapham. He was at the time a deserter from the R.A.F., and service police were on the look-out for him, with good evidence that he was hiding somewhere in South London. He went almost straight into the arms of the service police after he had strangled the woman, and he immediately followed the plan which had worked so successfully in the previous crime.

He said that his desertion was a minor matter compared with the crime he was about to admit—and he then gave a detailed confession of how he had murdered Beatrice Sutton.

This time the details were rather too comprehensive. Instead of making slight and deliberate errors which would later permit him to insist that he had been lying, he gave an authentic account which no one who had not been in that room of death could possibly have known.

He withdrew his confession as soon as the date of his Old Bailey trial was fixed, but it hardly mattered. The police confirmed with cold, hard facts item after item in his confession. Field was quickly found guilty and condemned to death.

In the legal record his motives remain indeterminable. Neither woman was robbed, although money and valuables were in their handbags. Neither body produced any medical evidence of sadistic injury before or after death. Neither woman had the slightest compunction about permitting intimacy.

But without any doubt Field suffered from a terrible sex aberration beyond the ken of normally-minded individuals. Neither the medical experts nor legal authorities could brand this monster as insane but he was without doubt abnormal in one tiny and terrible facet of his emotional make-up.

It was perhaps merely the kindly twist of fate that ensured Field's killings amounted only to two. For that the vanity which made him boast of his crimes must be thanked. His murders were so motiveless by all normal standards and so cunningly carried out that he would have stood a very good chance of going unpunished—as the first trial, with his own account of the murder freely given, indicated. But he was too vain. He simply had to see the world's reaction to his story—and that trait led him to the gallows.

If the motives which drove Frederick Field to murder lay hidden in the deep recesses of the emotions and produced an explanation which, if not understood, is at least tenable, there are no comprehensible reasons for the crime which brought Thomas Ley and Lawrence Smith to the

Old Bailey dock in 1947 in what has become known as the Chalk Pit Murder Case.

The character of greatest interest in this remarkable trial was Ley, not only because he was the mainspring of the bewildering events which led up to murder but because of his background.

I have said elsewhere that few murderers I have known have been wealthy men. Ley is the exception to prove the rule. He was one of the richest men to appear in the Old Bailey dock on any charge, and is, incidentally, the holder of the doubtful distinction of being the richest person ever to go to Broadmoor.

His life story is almost as bizarre as the crime which brought to an end his career. Born in England in 1881, Thomas Ley emigrated with his parents to Australia when he was nine years old. After the traditional beginnings of the self-made man—he sold newspapers at one time on the streets of Sydney—he became a clerk with a firm of solicitors and was soon a junior partner in the firm.

He began to dabble in politics in the suburb of Sydney, Kogarah, where he then lived, and in 1917 he won an electoral contest at Hurstville. Soon afterwards he was the leading personality in the Progressive Party and in 1922 was made Minister of Justice. Still only in his early forties he was universally regarded as the most formidable rival to Prime Minister Hughes, and only the turns and twists of political life prevented him becoming the leading political personality in Australia. He was known as Lemonade Ley because of his campaign to curb the sales and consumption of alcohol.

But there were certain vagaries in his career which aroused the suspicions of some of his colleagues and were responsible for a whispering campaign that soon precluded all real likelihood of his becoming head of the Government of Australia.

As Minister of Justice for New South Wales his political acumen could not be denied. Many legislative measures of the nineteen-twenties which improved the social conditions of the country were his work, but in minor matters he behaved in a most odd manner.

No one ever solved, for example, the mystery of the death of a business colleague—some said rival—whose body was found in the spring of 1928 at the bottom of the Coogie Cliffs in circumstances not really explained by accident or suicide.

There was also a complaint about some share pushing which, to say the least of it, was an inadvisable activity for a Minister of Justice. The really serious blot on his career came when a scandal arose about an election rival who had suddenly withdrawn from the contest, making Ley's success at the polls a foregone conclusion. The man concerned, when taxed with his absurd last-minute resignation, hinted at bribery. The scandal grew to such dimensions that the High Court of Australia announced that it would hold an official enquiry. It never took place because the chief witness simply disappeared. No one has ever discovered whether the man left the country or suffered some more ominous fate.

Perhaps wisely Ley accepted that the greatest rewards of political life were not to be his, and he more or less retired from active life, transferring his very considerable fortune to British and Continental banks. This was in 1930, and the name of Ley was forgotten in Australia until the murder case of 1946—except for a large studio photograph which hung on the wall of the Ministry of Justice, along with portraits of all the other holders of this illustrious office.

The Honourable Thomas Ley did not leave Australia alone. In a first-class cabin at a discreet distance from his own were a Mrs. Brooks and her daughter. Mrs. Brooks was his mistress, and the liaison had existed for years, although by the time of the murder the friendship was largely platonic, Mrs. Brooks then being in her middle sixties. Although living apart from his wife Ley was not completely estranged and husband and wife met at regular intervals in London and on the Riviera.

6

In due course Miss Brooks married a young man called Barron. They set up home in Wimbledon. The flat they took was part of a large house belonging to a Mrs. Evans who gained her living by letting rooms. One of her lodgers was a young barman from the Reigate Hill Hotel named Mudie. When Mrs. Barron fell ill her mother came round to look after her, and naturally Ley dropped in now and then to see how things were going.

And he did not like what he saw. For some reason that only his twisted brain could explain he suspected that his ageing mistress and the pleasant young barman were having an affair. He fixed on Mudie after indicating that he suspected Mrs. Brooks' son-in-law and another lodger in the house were also indulging in an illicit affair with a woman who could have been their grandmother. Having finally decided on Mudie as the snake in the grass he began to plan his fantastic murder.

First he found a hire car owner who indicated that he was ready to keep his mouth shut. This was a man named Buckingham. Next he had a chat with a carpenter who was working on some Kensington property of Ley's, Lawrence Smith.

The story he told to both of them was that he wanted to deal with a rogue who, after seducing a mother and her daughter, was blackmailing them. This gallant gesture may or may not have been accepted as the real facts by the two men. But the facts produced in evidence indicated that, whatever their real beliefs and however much they relied on the fact that Ley was a professional legal man who was fully aware of the niceties of the law, they were apparently unwilling to go to the police when they learned that the alleged blackmailer was to be kidnapped, preferring the large monetary rewards Ley offered.

After setting up his little gang Ley seemed to have decided to play cat-and-mouse with the unfortunate Mudie. First he took Mrs. Brooks away from the Wimbledon house and set her up in a flat in Kensington. Then he started a weird campaign to tempt the young man to go and see Mrs. Brooks, as if he wanted to torture himself with proof of his suspicions.

The very absence of any reaction from Mudie bred a frenzy in Ley's mind. With the help of a woman friend of Buckingham, who posed as a wealthy hostess who wanted Mudie to act as bartender at a private cocktail party, they got their prospective victim into a car and drove him to 5 Beaufort Gardens, S.W.7, a building which Ley owned and was converting into flats.

There Buckingham and Smith grabbed the unfortunate Mudie as he walked through the door. What happened thereafter is somewhat vague. Buckingham turned King's evidence, and all concerned did their best to wriggle out of the blame for the actual killing of Mudie.

But later that evening two cyclists saw a car standing inside the entrance to a chalk pit off Slines Oak Road, near Woldingham, Surrey. It was a miserable, wet night, and the two men might have thought that the car was a trysting place for lovers if they had not noticed in the gloom a man clambering towards the car down the slippery chalk sides of the quarry, and who leaped into the car and drove off.

They wondered about the car but did nothing for a couple of days. Then they read in the newspapers that a body had been found nearby. It had been discovered by a passer-by on the afternoon of November 29. The corpse was lying in an old army trench and a cord still remained around the neck. When the police came they found a pickaxe lying nearby and under the overcoat, which was tied round the body with a rope, was a piece of rag smelling of turpentine and shellac. Papers in the pocket of the dead man's suit gave the name of John Mudie of the Reigate Hill Hotel.

It was not long, of course, before the police learned something of Mudie's friends and visitors. The rag was traced to a decorator's toolbox at Beaufort Gardens, where the pickaxe had also been used for demolition work.

It was merely a question of sorting out which of the

peculiar characters in this tragic melodrama had been directly involved.

Ley, Smith and Buckingham were soon inside behind bars. Buckingham, who was an army deserter, made a cut-and-dried case even more certain by telling all he knew to Scotland Yard detectives, thereby saving his own skin. Smith, who made a very poor impression when he gave evidence on his own behalf and did his utmost to condemn Ley as the sole assailant, seems to have readily taken a leading part in this diabolical plan to destroy a harmless and likeable young man he had never met in his life, until Ley and Buckingham organised a meeting, for a reward of £300 in order to emigrate and set up in business in South Africa or New Zealand, was condemned to death.

Ley, a splendid-looking white haired man with the heavy jowls and folds of skin of a man who for years had lived in the lap of luxury might have found more sympathy with the jury if he had given evidence of the ridiculous suspicions about blackmail, seduction, and his plans for kidnapping. Instead he blandly stood in the witness box and in full rich tones, with only a slight trace of an Australian accent, denied everything, even incidents which had been proved up to the hilt.

He had the slightly surprised look of the true lunatic who is utterly convinced that everyone but himself is insane and he the only person with the vestige of mental acumen, as his counsel, Sir Walter Monckton, tried to do the best he could for his client. Ley was the sort of man who would have told the Lord High Justice himself—and he was the judge at this trial—that black is white and become nettled that his Lordship could believe otherwise.

Mad Ley was, but mad in the legal sense at the time he helped in that horrible attack in an empty room on a man who imagined he was stepping into a salon to be used for a cocktail party, he was not. The Judge could do nothing but sentence Ley to death and then let the processes of the law order the prisoner's medical examination.

This, as was expected, resulted in Ley being declared a

paranoic and Broadmoor's gates opened to receive another travesty of a human being. Seven weeks later the Honourable Thomas Ley had a heart attack and died in the mercy of inscrutable Providence.

My last "strange case" memory is one of those comparatively rare instances of a still unsolved murder mystery where clues to the crime were sufficient to warrant a charge.

There are, of course, many murders where the police are unable to present evidence to justify an arrest, but the truly mystifying case where a trial is held yet fails to probe the real facts is unusual.

In saying this I am not talking about a case like that of the dead Nora Upchurch. In such cases it may be fairly obvious where the guilt lies, even if it cannot be legally proved. The trial I am about to relate was not like this. It contained—and still contains—elements of mystery which are intriguing.

The amazing trial of a man named Hume for murder began on January 18, 1950, before Mr. Justice Lewis. My memory of the evidence remains unusually clear for most of it was given twice. After a score of witnesses had appeared for the prosecution the judge fell ill, and the proceedings began all over again before Mr. Justice Sellers.

The story which emerged was a revelation of the half-world of the black market which existed in those days of austerity. It began when a man called at a police station to report that a relative of his, Stanley Setty, had been missing for two days. Setty was a motor trader operating in the streets and showrooms around Warren Street. At the time cars were, of course, in short supply, with second-hand vehicles of recent make fetching far above the list price for new models.

It was quickly discovered that Setty had completed a cash deal on the evening that he was last seen and must have had more than £1,000 in £5 notes in his possession, for the banks were shut when he sold the car and received payment.

Despite the most widespread search no trace whatever of his movements after he had driven off down the Euston Road with the intention of visiting his sister for dinner could be discovered. Then, a fortnight later, a wildfowler punting across the sea marshes at Tillingham, Essex, found a large bundle wrapped in grey felt and tied with ropes. He cut the rope and to his horror saw a human body inside.

Police sent the body and its wrappings to Scotland Yard. The head and legs were missing. There were stab wounds in the chest. The fact that almost every bone was broken indicated that the body had been subjected to great violence, but had not been subjected to prolonged pressure.

The murderer or murderers had been foolish to leave the corpse's arms on the torso. Fingerprints were taken and it was found that they were on Scotland Yard's files. They belonged to Stanley Setty, who had been in prison for fraud twenty years before.

The area where the body had been found and the fact that the bones had been fractured suggested that it had been dumped from an aircraft. Confirmation that this theory was probably the right one came with news from the staff at Elstree aerodrome that a man had three weeks earlier hired a small plane, taken a large bundle from his car and dumped it in the fuselage, and had taken off. His hiring arrangement gave the details that he intended to fly to Southend.

At Southend airport a man was found who recalled a plane landing late on the afternoon of the day in question, the man concerned saying he would return on the following day. He had then hired a car to be driven to London. The driver of this car was found. He remembered his fare paying with a £5 note taken from a bundle.

Witnesses and the airport records at Southend showed that the plane had been flown off on the following day, October 6, ostensibly for Elstree. A large parcel was transferred from a car to the plane before the plane left.

But the plane did not arrive back at Elstree that day. It had landed at Gravesend, where once again the pilot had hired a car to be driven to London. This driver was also paid with a £5 note.

The pilot made no effort to conceal his identity, as indeed with the formalities of showing his licence and so on he could not have done. He was stated by the various witnesses to be named Brian Donald Hume.

Interviewed at his Finchley home, Hume at first denied everything. Eventually he agreed to talk. His story was that two men had got into conversation with him in the kerbside motor market of Warren Street on September 30. All he knew about them was that they were called Mac and Green. They had discovered that he was a licensed pilot and they put up a scheme for smuggling which, they said, would be worth £50 to him.

Hume agreed, and on the next day Mac and Green, with another individual they called Boy, arrived at his home with two large bundles. They said that they were the plates used for forging petrol coupons and they wanted them dumped in the sea. Hume shoved the bundles in a kitchen cupboard and then made enquiries about hiring a plane. A few hours later he drove to Elstree. The next part of his story confirmed what the police had already discovered about his movements on the first day.

Then he explained what had happened after he reached London from Southend. Mac was waiting him at his home to learn how he had got on. Hearing that he had been successful he then took him outside and in a car parked at the corner of the street, in which Green and Boy were sitting, was a still larger parcel. This was also to be dumped in the sea—fee £100, cash in advance.

Hume agreed and the bundle was carried indoors and put in the kitchen cupboard. He admitted that he suspected this parcel contained a body, and even that it was Setty's, who was a business friend, for whom he by then knew the police were searching. Nevertheless he quite calmly went on with his plans. When later a check of the numbers of £5 notes with which he had been paid showed that they tallied with those issued to the Press by the police, he was, of course, virtually certain of the crime in which he had become involved.

But a menacing phone call from someone whom he recognised as Boy warned him that he would be wise to keep his mouth shut.

Despite the most ruthless comb-out of the area and the questioning of scores of people the police could find no trace whatever of Green, Mac and Boy.

Hume was thereupon charged with murder.

The prosecution had a massive array of evidence against him—but it was mostly circumstantial. A considerable amount of blood was found in Hume's house. It existed on the carpet, although this had been recently cleaned and dyed ; there were traces in the cracks of the kitchen floorboards, on the linoleum in the hall, on the stairs leading to the bathroom, and on the floor of the fuselage of the aircraft Hume had flown. But it was Group O blood, and although this was Setty's group, it is also the group of nearly half the population. Some blood had been spilled in Hume's flat, but it was not necessarily Setty's.

Hume lived in a crowded residential area. Cutting the legs off a corpse is a prolonged and invariably noisy business. No other tenant in the house had heard anything ; no one had noticed a large and cumbersome parcel —and Setty was a biggish man—being carried into the flat on the night when the corpse must have been cut up.

The pathologist, Dr. Teare, who gave medical evidence, said that he believed more than one person must have been concerned in the murder. And despite the failure of the police to find any trace of the mysterious trio of Mac, Green and Boy in the Warren Street area a journalist did come forward to say that he had met Mac and Boy in Paris a month or two before the murder.

Hume elected to give evidence on his own behalf. I felt that he made a good appearance considering the terrible weight of evidence against him, and he made no pretence of excusing himself for participating in a vile and horrible conspiracy just as he vehemently denied that he had been the actual assailant.

It was one of those cases where it was anybody's guess as to what the verdict would be. The Judge's impartial summing up gave the facts, and to my mind, as I think to everyone who was an onlooker at that trial, the jury had a formidable task to sift the truth from the welter of evidence, to take an objective view of facts without being biased by the natural loathing for the callousness of the young man in the dock.

And so it proved. After two and a half hours the foreman said that they could not reach a decision, and it was doubtless perfectly reasonable to accept that no matter how long they conferred they would never agree.

At the new trial no evidence was offered on the charge of murder and Hume was charged with being an accessory after the fact. On this, by his own evidence, there could be no doubt that he was guilty, and he received a sentence of twelve years' imprisonment.

The law had ordained that Hume did not kill Setty, and I believe that the law was right. The mystery remains as to how the victim was lured to his doom, how the murder was achieved so secretively and so efficiently, and how many people were involved in it.

It was, I think, the first case in which the use of an aircraft to overcome that terrible obstacle which besets all murderers—the disposal of the body—was revealed. It was also a strange case in that the prisoner endured the awful experience of an Old Bailey trial for almost three times as long as normal—the proceedings terminated by the Judge's illness, the resumed case before a new Judge, and then the trial on the lesser charge.

CHAPTER ELEVEN

Upholding the Law

MY MEMORIES CONTINUE TO CROWD IN ON me, for I have been able to recount only a minute fraction of the trials that have occurred in over half a century of Old Bailey history. I find that few people whose activities have no connexion with the legal profession or the enforcement of law and order have any conception of the formidable total of crime which our Courts have to deal with ; this is not to say that Great Britain is a lawless country. On the contrary, our figures of offences against the law compare very favourably with those of any nation on earth, and the proportion of offenders who are brought to justice is the envy of every other country.

But with a population of fifty millions it will be obvious that serious crime—that is to say indictable offences not triable summarily and falling into the three categories of treason, felony and misdemeanour—must always be a serious factor.

Since my career began the number of persons tried at the Assizes and Quarter Sessions in England and Wales (which include the Central Criminal Court) has more than doubled. The post-war average is just under 20,000 per year.

Newspaper readers know virtually nothing about the major proportion of these cases. They are not reported for the simple reason that even to deal with a single day's hearings adequately would fill the ordinary newspaper from the first page to the last.

For the purpose of official records the offences which take people into the dock of the Old Bailey and those in the provincial Assize and Sessions Courts are classified in groups.

In Class One (offences against the person) there are

twenty-six offences, ranging from murder and man-slaughter to incest and bigamy. In Class Two (offences against property with violence) there are nine offences, including sacrilege, burglary and blackmail. Class Three accounts for thousands of trials every year: it covers offences against property without violence, and includes embezzlement, larceny and fraud. Class Four brings comparatively few cases. It covers malicious injuries to property, which usually mean arson. Forgery is the main offence in Class Five, and the final Class covers comparatively rare offences such as treason, riot, perjury, attempted suicide, bribery of voters and other election offences.

It is small wonder that the majority of these cases are of brief duration, little public interest, and of never-ceasing incidence. They are examples of the exhausting toil which Her Majesty's judges, counsel, solicitors and court officials endure day after day. These thousands of cases are the real work of the judicature, not the spectacular murder trials which last for days and permit counsel and witnesses to appear in the full limelight of national interest.

But it must be remembered that these day-to-day cases are the difficult ones. All the experience and acumen of the legal folk involved have to be brought to bear on a case of shopbreaking just as much as in a trial for mass murder. The accused is entitled to the full benefits of justice irrespective of the seriousness of his offence.

I have heard prolonged legal arguments involving the presence of numerous expert witnesses and the adjournment of the hearing while references are consulted in a case which concerned the larceny of a couple of post letters, and I have seen a murderer who has pleaded guilty have his case disposed of in a matter of minutes.

It cannot be stressed too strongly that there is no one working in the Court for any reason except to see that justice is done. Prosecuting counsel are not there just for the purpose of securing conviction, nor defence counsel to see that a guilty person gets off. Nor have I ever known a judge who showed any personal bias, unjustified tolerance or unreasonable severity.

The Press has from time to time dubbed a judge as "a Hanging Judge"—Mr. Justice Avory was one of them —and always the description is very unfair. No one who knew Avory could think of him except as a man whose outlook was gentle and forgiving. If he indicated in his summing up and sentence his implacable loathing of some brutish monster guilty of murder and therefore with his life forfeit to society, there were scores of times when his pity for a prisoner showed that his passion for justice could always be tempered with mercy.

I have seen him near to tears as he tried to reassure some unfortunate girl found guilty of infanticide that the law would help as well as punish her, and only prisoners' families and the charitable organisations connected with the rescue work among the criminal classes can tell of the amount of aid he, like so many judges, provided.

The red-robed criminal judge of the Old Bailey, sitting on the bench to hear the long procession of cases in the twelve sessions which continue year in and year out, could well be forgiven if he lost all faith in human decency. That he does not is testimony to his humanity.

I am often asked whether in my experience the characters of the tens of thousands of men and women who have moved in and out of the dock of the Courts of Old Bailey in the past fifty years have changed. My answer is that everything about them has changed greatly.

When I first went to work there was a very definite criminal class. Burglars, housebreakers and petty thieves were incorrigible rogues who appeared in Court time after time, almost as soon after they were out of prison. They were uneducated, dirty and shabby. They were as identifiable as the character of Bill Sikes in Dickens.

The woman criminal was a comparatively rare personality. She was always very obviously what she was, and if she made a pretence of injured innocence at first it soon disappeared and the virago underneath asserted itself.

Today, even in proportion to the increase in population crime is not much more serious than it used to be, but the criminal is part of every class in society. The master burglar may be a meek little man, neatly dressed and diffident, like a minor shopkeeper. The sexual offender is quite likely to be a bank clerk, civil servant or similarly hitherto highly respected member of the community. Women criminals, young and old, come from every class and no one could possibly identify them for what they are from a chance meeting. The pretty young woman who looks like a City secretary may be a member of a ruthless blackmail gang ; the middle-aged woman dressed and behaving like a suburban housewife is revealed as a " madame " battening on scores of unfortunate girls.

Crime, I am afraid, has become almost respectable. " Thou Shalt Not Be Caught " is the only commandment that matters. Social ostracism for dishonesty, anti-social behaviour, and even cruelty is at the best temporary.

But the biggest change that I have seen is in the behaviour of counsel. My first years at the Old Bailey coincided with what has been decribed as the golden era of English advocacy. The interminable and dreary speeches of the Victorian era (sometimes proceedings continued until midnight and after) had given way to brilliant rhetoric, with invective and epigram providing a glittering aura to the hearing.

Whether these advocates helped the dignity of the Court as much as they raised the standard of forensic artistry is open to doubt. I remember the open enmity which existed between Mr. Justice Mathew and the brilliant but hot-tempered Marshall Hall. The insults that the famous advocate hurled at the bench would never be tolerated today, nor indeed would they be voiced by any Q.C. And I remember the rapier-like thrusts of the famous F. E. Smith (Lord Birkenhead), whom we called the D'Artagnan of the Law, when he was annoyed by some ruling of the Judge.

These scenes have gone, not because there is no more

brilliance among counsel, but because it is out of fashion. I think perhaps Sir Patrick Hastings was the last of a wonderful line.

Of the judges I have been privileged to know my earliest memory is of Mr. Justice Grantham, who used to ride to Court on a white horse. He was a kindly man who loved the good things of life, and it was his occasional practice to invite a few younger barristers to lunch with him during the session. A traditional item at this meal was rum punch, and it was sometimes quite obvious that some of his guests hardly had the head for this brew. Incidentally, the abstemious habits of today certainly did not always prevail fifty years ago, and slurred speech, untidy dress, and hot tempers were symptoms of a very good luncheon during afternoon proceedings.

Now the judges are quite likely to drive up in a small car driven by a member of the family, or by taxicab. But their majestic remoteness has not changed. The Lords Chief Justice of recent times—Lord Hewart and Lord Goddard—will without doubt be named by future generations of lawyers as among the half dozen most illustrious names in English jurisprudence.

Lastly, what of that vital part of every case—the jury? Jurymen and women are today, I think, far more intelligent and much more conscious of their responsibilities.

I have seen the number of the jury reduced to seven, as it was during the war, and I have heard legal opinions, as for example that of the Lord Chief Justice speaking during the ceremony of the Lord Mayor's Oath in 1953, suggesting this be continued or of accepting a majority verdict.

Convenient as such proposals might be to speed up and economise on administration of justice, it is doubtful whether they will be adopted. The priceless safeguard which every defendant at the Old Bailey and any other Assize Court enjoys is the fact that the doubts of just one person out of twelve ordinary, decent men and women will beyond all doubt prevent his punishment.

" The correctness of a jury's verdict has almost come to

be an axiom with me," Mr. Justice Travers Humphreys once said, and I believe that all lawyers and judges would concur.

The public may sometimes think that a jury is too tender-hearted and is too prone to give a prisoner the benefit of the doubt. If there is anything in this belief it does not mean that there is any miscarriage of justice.

It is possible that there may be a wrongful conviction, and the Court of Criminal Appeal exists to remedy this. But there has never been, and never can be, a wrongful acquittal. It must be remembered that the jury is not asked to convince itself of an accused person's innocence but to be certain of his guilt. It may well feel very doubtful that the prisoner they have watched in the dock is innocent, but that must not prevent them believing that the prosecution has failed to prove his guilt and that therefore he is entitled to go free.

Over the years I have conducted many famous persons from overseas to a privileged seat in the Old Bailey courts. They have come from every country in the world to watch the administration of justice in the most famous of all criminal courts. They have listened to the quaint terms of the age-old ceremonial, observed the impressiveness of the judges in their scarlet and ermine, listened to men whose brilliant loquacity is a byword—but nearly always they have, in summing up their impressions afterwards, first paid tribute to the behaviour of the jury.

I always used to take them to see a marble tablet which was placed in a wall of one of the rooms damaged during the blitz. It recorded that:

Near this site
William Penn and William Mead were tried in 1670 for preaching to an unlawful assembly in Gracechurch Street.
This tablet commemorates the courage and endurance of the jury, Thomas Vere, Edward Bushell and ten others who refused to give a verdict against them, although locked up without food for two nights and were fined for their final verdict of Not Guilty.

THE GUILTY AND THE INNOCENT

The story of the Old Bailey, with all its tragedy, is really the story of the ordinary people who have since the days of William the Conqueror shouldered the responsibility of trying their fellow citizens.

That Justice stands, eyes open and impartial, atop the building unassailed and unassailable, is testimony to the incorruptibility of twelve ordinary citizens who, by a twist of fate, have been brought together to share the responsibility of deciding the fate of another—between freedom and imprisonment, life and death.

THE END.